SHAKESPEARE ON LOVE

JOSEPH PEARCE

SHAKESPEARE ON LOVE

Seeing the Catholic Presence in
Romeo and Juliet

IGNATIUS PRESS   SAN FRANCISCO

Cover photo
Juliet's Balcony, by Milo Persic
According to local tradition, this house in Verona, Italy,
belonged to the family
that served as Shakespeare's inspiration for the Capulets.

Cover design by Milo Persic

© 2013 by Ignatius Press, San Francisco
All rights reserved
ISBN 978-1-58617-684-6
Library of Congress Control Number 2012942805
Printed in the United States of America ∞

FOR LORNA
WITH
LOVE

CONTENTS

PREFACE

This book rests on the solid conviction that William Shakespeare was a believing Catholic. The evidence for such a conviction has been given in my two previous books *The Quest for Shakespeare* and *Through Shakespeare's Eyes*. In the first of these volumes the solid documentary and biographical evidence for the Bard's Catholicism is given; in the latter the evidence for his Catholicism is gleaned from three of his most celebrated plays, *The Merchant of Venice*, *Hamlet*, and *King Lear*. It should be stated from the outset, therefore, that these other books should be consulted for the definitive proof of Shakespeare's Catholic faith, whereas the present volume will simply offer further corroboration of the conclusions reached in the earlier volumes, based on the evidence that emerges in *Romeo and Juliet*, his most popular play and perhaps the most famous tragedy ever written.

It should also be stressed that the belief in Shakespeare's Catholicism is not simply an eccentric and quixotic quest on the part of the present author but is a firmly established field of scholarship. Apart from my own two contributions to the burgeoning library of books on the subject, I will list here some of the most noteworthy.

The Shakespeares and "The Old Faith" by John Henry De Groot is a meticulously researched study of the Catholicism of Shakespeare's family by a Protestant scholar.[1] Carol Curt Enos' *Shakespeare and the Catholic Religion* is an accessible

[1] John Henry De Groot, *The Shakespeares and "The Old Faith"* (Fraser, Mich.: Real-View Books, 1995); originally published in 1946.

summary of much of the most salient evidence.[2] Peter Milward's many works exhibit the fruits of a life of devoted scholarship. It would take more space than would be appropriate in this short summary to list all of his work on the subject, but those particularly worthy of attention are *Shakespeare's Religious Background, The Catholicism of Shakespeare's Plays, Shakespeare the Papist, Elizabethan Shakespeare,* and *Jacobean Shakespeare.*[3] Perhaps the most compendious study of the whole issue is *Shakespeare and Catholicism,* a monumental work by two German scholars, Heinrich Mutschmann and Karl Wentersdorf.[4] More recently, another fine German scholar, Hildegard Hammerschmidt-Hummel, has been causing controversy and gaining international headlines for her groundbreaking discoveries. Although she has written several works on the subject of Shakespeare's faith, her panoramic overview of the whole issue is given in *The Life and Times of William Shakespeare.*[5] The pioneering study, which blazed the trail for much that followed, was *The Religion of Shakespeare* by Richard Simpson, published in 1899.[6] *Shakespeare and the Culture of Christianity in Early Modern England,* edited by Dennis Taylor and David N. Beauregard, contains

[2] Carol Curt Enos, *Shakespeare and the Catholic Religion* (Pittsburgh: Dorrance, 2000).

[3] Peter Milward, *Shakespeare's Religious Background* (Chicago: Loyola University Press, 1973); *The Catholicism of Shakespeare's Plays* (London: Saint Austin Press, 2000); *Shakespeare the Papist* (Ave Maria. Fla.: Sapientia Press, 2005); *Elizabethan Shakespeare* (Ave Maria, Fla.: Sapientia Press, 2007); and *Jacobean Shakespeare* (Ave Maria, Fla: Sapientia Press, 2007).

[4] Heinrich Mutschmann and Karl Wentersdorf, *Shakespeare and Catholicism* (New York: Sheed and Ward, 1952).

[5] Hildegard Hammerschmidt-Hummel, *The Life and Times of William Shakespeare 1664–1616* (London: Chaucer Press, 2007).

[6] Richard Simpson and Henry Sebastian Bowden, *The Religion of Shakespeare: Chiefly from the Writings of the Late Mr. Richard Simpson, M.A.* (London: Burns & Oates, 1899).

many insightful essays, and Ian Wilson's *Shakespeare: The Evidence* argues the case for the Bard's Catholicism with incisive and persuasive aplomb.[7]

The foregoing list is not by any means exhaustive, and those seeking a more thoroughgoing bibliographical grounding in the expansive and expanding body of scholarship in this area should check the bibliography in the aforementioned *Quest for Shakespeare*.[8] The point, however, is that Shakespeare was a believing Catholic when he wrote his plays, *Romeo and Juliet* included, and, as such, we should expect to find the presence of the faith, philosophically and theologically, in the midst of this greatest of love stories. Seeing the tragedy unfold through Shakespeare's Catholic eyes enables us to see it in a new and surprising light. The following work is an effort to see the play through the eyes of the playwright so that we may be enlightened and surprised by what we see.

[7] Dennis Taylor and David N. Beauregard, eds., *Shakespeare and the Culture of Christianity in Early Modern England* (New York: Fordham University Press, 2003); Ian Wilson, *Shakespeare: The Evidence; Unlocking the Mysteries of the Man and His Work* (New York: St. Martin's Griffin, 1994).

[8] Joseph Pearce, *The Quest for Shakespeare: The Bard of Avon and the Church of Rome* (San Francisco: Ignatius, 2008).

ACKNOWLEDGMENTS

For the most part, this book is simply an engagement with the text of Shakespeare's most famous play. As such, there are not too many people to acknowledge in the traditional sense in which such people are listed at the beginning of a book. I could and should list those people who have inspired and encouraged me in my love for Shakespeare and the research which is its fruit. Since, however, I listed these people in the acknowledgments of my previous book, *Through Shakespeare's Eyes*, I shall desist from repeating myself on this occasion, which is not to say, of course, that I am any the less indebted to them.

In writing this book, I have gained much from my experience of editing the Ignatius Critical Edition of *Romeo and Juliet*, published in 2011, and from the insights gleaned from other contributors to that edition, particularly Crystal Downing, Richard Harp, Andrew J. Harvey, Jill Kriegel, Jonathan Marks, Rebecca Munro, and Stephen Zelnick.

It would be remiss of me, and indeed an act of the grossest negligence and ingratitude, were I not to mention those valued benefactors and encouragers of my work at Thomas More College and Ignatius Press who continue to make it possible for me to write and publish my work.

Aptly enough, the final acknowledgment of gratitude belongs to my wife, Susannah. Apart from reading and critiquing every chapter of the present volume as it was written, she has to take on that much greater burden of living with me and my idiosyncrasies. Only through the grace of God can such crosses be borne!

PROLOGUE:
THE GREATEST LOVE STORY EVER TOLD?

In the history of the world, and in the canon of world literature, there have been many great love affairs and many legendary lovers. We think perhaps of Helen and Paris, Odysseus and Penelope, Aeneas and Dido, Antony and Cleopatra, Dante and Beatrice, Paolo and Francesca, Petrarch and Laura. And, of course, whenever we think of the world's greatest lovers we can scarcely avoid thinking of Romeo and Juliet. Yet when we step back from the list we notice something a little odd about the lovers and their love affairs. We are struck by how different one love affair is from another. On the one hand we have the adulterous passion of Helen and Paris, with its destructive consequences; on the other, we have the loyalty and chastity of the devoted wife Penelope, who serves as a beacon of light on her husband's dark journey home. We have the disastrous love affairs of Aeneas and Dido, and Antony and Cleopatra, in which the lovers are so obsessed with each other that they forget and neglect their duties to their family, friends, and country. We have the adulterous love of Paolo and Francesca that leads to the murder of Francesca's husband and the hurtling of the lovers into the hell of their infernal passion. At the other end of the lovers' spectrum we have Petrarch's idealized love for the unattainable Laura, and Dante's idealized love for Beatrice, the latter of which, stripped of all selfishness, baptizes Dante's imagination, enabling him to ascend to the mystic heights of beatitude. Thus we see that the right sort of love can lead us to heaven, whereas the wrong sort can condemn us to hell. If this is so, what sort of love do Romeo and Juliet have for each other? Is their love the right sort or the wrong sort? Is it heavenly or hellish? Is it fruitful or destructive?

Romeo and Juliet is perhaps the most famous love story ever written. Its cultural influence is so profound that Shakespeare's "star cross'd" lovers have become synonymous with the very meaning of romantic love. But what exactly does the world's greatest playwright have to say about the world's greatest lovers? Does he sympathize with their plight? Does he consider them blameless, or are they at least partly responsible for the tragedy that awaits them? Is the love story about fatalistic forces beyond the control of the protagonists, or is it a cautionary tale warning of the dangers of unbridled erotic passion? And what does Shakespeare have to say about the relationship between romantic love, or eros, and the greatest love of all, the love which God has for man, which manifests itself in his giving his only Son as a willing sacrifice for man's salvation? What relationship is there between eros and caritas, between the romantic love between a man and a woman and the love of Christ for humanity? What is the connection between the most famous love story ever written and the Greatest Love that there is? These questions are asked and answered in the following pages as we endeavor to see *Romeo and Juliet* through Shakespeare's devoutly Catholic eyes.

I

CREATIVE REVISION AND
CRITICAL MISREADING

As with so many of Shakespeare's plays, the exact date of
Romeo and Juliet's composition is shrouded in mystery and
is the cause of much scholarly argument and disagreement.
When it appeared in print for the first time, in 1597, the
title page referred to its being performed "with great
applause" by Lord Hunsdon's Men. Since Shakespeare's acting troupe was known as Lord Hunsdon's Men only between
July 1596 and March 1597 it is assumed, logically enough,
that the play must have been written in 1595 or 1596. Some
scholars believe, however, that it was written as early as 1591,
arguing that the Nurse's remark " 'Tis since the earthquake
now eleven years" (1.3.24)[1] constitutes a clear allusion to
the London earthquake of 1580. Countering such a suggestion, advocates of the later date refer to William Covell's
Polimanteia, a work with which they presume Shakespeare
was aware, that alludes to an earthquake of 1584.

Much less controversial than the dating of the play is the
principal source upon which it is based. All critics seem to

---

[1] All quotes from *Romeo and Juliet* are taken from William Shakespeare,
Romeo and Juliet, ed. Joseph Pearce, Ignatius Critical Editions (San Francisco:
Ignatius Press, 2011).

agree that the main wellspring of Shakespeare's inspiration for *Romeo and Juliet* was Arthur Brooke's long poem, *The Tragicall Historye of Romeus and Juliet*, published in 1562. Although Brooke was himself indebted to a tradition of romantic tragedies emanating from the Italian Renaissance, it seems that the essential ingredients of Shakespeare's play are taken from Brooke's poem. Since Shakespeare's modus operandi often involved the confuting of his sources, correcting their anti-Catholic biases with modes of expression more conducive to his own beliefs, it is worth looking at Brooke's poem in order to see what it is that Shakespeare does to it. Before doing so, we should remind ourselves that this "correcting" of the anti-Catholic prejudices of his sources is something with which Shakespeare would remain preoccupied.

Shortly before embarking upon the writing of *Romeo and Juliet*, Shakespeare had written his play *King John* as a reaction against the anti-Catholic bias of an earlier play entitled *The Troublesome Reign of King John*. A few years later, Shakespeare wrote *Hamlet* in response to an earlier play, that scholars now call the *Ur-Hamlet*, which was probably written by Thomas Kyd. Although Kyd's play has been lost to posterity, the fact that Kyd had been tried and imprisoned for atheism in 1593 could suggest that Shakespeare had sought to "baptize" the story of Hamlet with his own profoundly Christian imagination. This revisiting of older works to correct their defects was employed once again in the writing of *King Lear*, in which Shakespeare counters the anti-Catholic bias of an earlier play, *The True Chronicle History of King Leir and His Three Daughters*, which was probably written by George Peele, and also in Shakespeare's writing of *Macbeth* to comment upon an earlier play on a similar theme, *The Tragedy of Gowrie*, which had been banned, presumably by direct order of the king himself. Since this process of creative revisionism (to give it a name) seems part of Shakespeare's inspirational motivation in selecting a theme upon which to write, it would be a sin of critical omission to fail to examine how Shakespeare's play confutes the bias of its source.

The bias of Arthur Brooke's *Tragicall Historye of Romeus and Juliet* is scarcely difficult to detect. On the contrary, the poem wears its author's Puritanism and anti-Catholicism on its sleeve, and emblazons it across its proud and prejudiced chest:

> To this ende (good Reader) is this tragicall matter written, to describe unto thee a coople of unfortunate lovers, thralling themselves to unhonest desire, neglecting the authoritie and advise of parents and frendes, conferring their principall counsels with dronken gossyppes, and superstitious friers (the naturally fitte instruments of unchastitie) attemptyng all adventures of peryll, for th'attaynyng of their wished lust, using auriculer confession (the kay of whoredome, and treason) for furtheraunce of theyre purpose, abusying the honorable name of lawefull marriage, the cloke the shame of stolne contractes, finallye, by all means of unhonest lyfe, hastyng to most unhappy deathe.[2]

In reading Brooke's puritanical preface we are struck instantly by his judgmentalism and by his anti-Catholicism. Brooke's Juliet is a "wily wench" waxing merry over her successful deception of her mother, and his Friar is indeed superstitious and a naturally fit instrument of unchastity, practicing treason and encouraging whoredom. Whereas Brooke emerges as the Pharisee who is ready to stone the wanton sinners to death, urging his readers to do likewise, perhaps

---

[2] From the original preface of Arthur Brooke's *Tragicall Historye of Romeus and Juliet* (London, 1562).

by means of a no-popery riot, Shakespeare, in his wonderful reworking of the tragedy, echoes Christ's response to the Pharisee, asking the one without sin to cast the first stone but also, crucially, reminding the sinners, on the stage and in the audience, to go and sin no more. Indeed, it is not that Shakespeare discards all morality in his own telling of the tale, contrary to the apparent belief of many of today's postmodern critics; it is simply that he removes the rabid anti-Catholicism, the Puritanism, and the sort of preachy propagandizing that belongs in the pulpit, perhaps, but not in the finest of art. As such, Christ's riposte to the Pharisee is a fitting metaphor for Shakespeare's riposte to Brooke.

Having discussed the original source and motivation for Shakespeare's writing of *Romeo and Juliet*, let's proceed to a discussion of the play itself.

Broadly speaking, it seems that there are three ways of reading the play. The first is the fatalistic reading in which fate or fortune are perceived as omnipotent but blind and impersonal forces which crush the "star-cross'd lovers", and everyone else, with mechanical indifference. In such a reading, free will, if it exists at all, is utterly powerless to resist intractable Fate. If the fatalistic reading is accepted, nobody is to blame for the events that unfold throughout the play because there is nothing anyone can do to alter them.

The second way of reading the play is what may be termed the "feudal" [3] or romantic reading, in which the feuding

---

[3] I am taking linguistic liberties, creating a neologism based etymologically upon the Old English *fæhthu* (enmity), from which "feud" is derived, as distinct from the common usage of "feudal", which has its roots in the Latin *feodum, feudum*, from which "feudal", "fee", and "fief" are derived, possibly from the original Frankish *fehod* (cattle-property). See the *Concise Oxford Dictionary of Current English*, 5th edition (Oxford: Oxford University Press, 1964).

parties are held to blame for the tragic fate of the doom-struck and love-struck lovers. In such a reading, the hatred and bigotry of the Capulets and Montagues are the primary cause of all the woes, and the lovers are hapless victims of their parents' bloodlust who are nonetheless redeemed and purified by the passion and purity of their love for each other. In our day and age, this is perhaps the most widely accepted interpretation of the play's overarching morality or deepest meaning, harmonizing as it does with the ingrained roman-ticism and narcissism of the zeitgeist. Such a reading allows our contemporary epoch to moralize about "love" and "hate" without the imposition of conventional moral norms. It is the morality of Lennon's "All You Need Is Love", a "love" which is rooted in the gratification of desire and which has its antecedents in the romanticism of Byronic self-indulgence.

The third way of reading the play is the cautionary or moral reading in which the freely chosen actions of each of the characters are seen to have far-ranging and far-reaching consequences. In such a reading, the animosity of the feud-ing parties and its consequences are weighed alongside the actions of the lovers, and those of other significant charac-ters, such as Friar Lawrence, Benvolio, Mercutio, the Prince, and the Nurse. Each is perceived and judged according to his actions and the consequences of those actions on others, and each is integrated into the whole picture so that the overriding and overarching moral may emerge. It is surely significant, for instance, that *Romeo and Juliet* was probably written at around the same time as *The Merchant of Venice*, a play that is preoccupied with the whole question of freedom of choice and its consequences.[4] Clearly such questions were

---

[4] *The Merchant of Venice* was probably written in late 1594 or, more likely, in 1595. As discussed already, the most likely date for the writing of *Romeo*

at the forefront of the playwright's mind as he grappled with the hateful or besotted choices of his Veronese protagonists as they had been when he grappled with the choices facing his Venetian heroes and villains.

In spite of the misreadings of many modern critics, it is clear from *Romeo and Juliet* itself, and from its place within the wider Shakespearean canon, that the only correct way of reading the play is the third way. It is, however, not the present writer who affirms this as an opinion, but the play itself that insists upon it as a fact.

---

and Juliet is 1595 or possibly 1596. For a full discussion of the role of choice and its consequences in *The Merchant of Venice*, see Joseph Pearce, *Through Shakespeare's Eyes: Seeing the Catholic Presence in the Plays* (San Francisco: Ignatius Press, 2010), chapters 6 and 7.

2

ROMEO: "A MADNESS MOST DISCREET"

There is perhaps no better way to begin an investigation into *Romeo and Juliet* than with the timelessly astute words of Samuel Taylor Coleridge:

> Shakespeare knew the human mind, and its most minute and intimate workings, and he never introduces a word, or a thought, in vain or out of place: if we do not understand him, it is our own fault or the fault of copyists and typographers; but study, and the possession of some small stock of the knowledge by which he worked, will enable us often to detect and explain his meaning. He never wrote at random, or hit upon points of character and conduct by chance; and the smallest fragment of his mind not unfrequently gives a clue to a most perfect, regular, and consistent whole.[1]

Although these words of Coleridge are equally applicable to any of the Bard's works, it is significant that they were written in relation to *Romeo and Juliet* in particular. With this in mind, let's read the play desiring to "detect and explain" Shakespeare's meaning in the light of the "most perfect, regular, and consistent whole" that he presents to us.

[1] Samuel Taylor Coleridge, *Shakespearean Criticism* (London: W. Pickering, 1849), p. 433.

The play's opening scene shows us, in no uncertain terms, the ugliness of the world in which Romeo and Juliet are living. Sampson and Gregory, two servants of the house of Capulet, revel in the rivalry between the Capulets and their Montague enemies and indulge in salacious and uncouth reveries in which they fantasize about the rape of the Montague women. Thus the vicious vindictiveness of the "ancient grudge" between the two noble households is exposed in the vile vernacular of their servants. The presence of such hatred is, however, merely the backdrop to the play's depiction of "love", or that which purports to be love but which is, in fact, a false and fallacious parody of it.

This false and fallacious love is first brought to our attention by Montague, Romeo's father, in his description of his son's odd behavior:

> Many a morning hath he there been seen,
> With tears augmenting the fresh morning's dew,
> Adding to clouds more clouds with his deep sighs;
> But all so soon as the all-cheering sun
> Should in the farthest east begin to draw
> The shady curtains from Aurora's bed,
> Away from light steals home my heavy son,
> And private in his chamber pens himself,
> Shuts up his windows, locks fair daylight out,
> And makes himself an artificial night.
> Black and portentous must this humour prove,
> Unless good counsel may the cause remove.
>
> (1.1.129–40)

Simultaneous with the introduction of the theme of false love is the introduction of the prevailing metaphor of light-shunning darkness which Shakespeare will employ throughout the play's entirety. Self-obsessed and obsessive "love" is an enemy of the light, making of itself "an artificial night", locking itself into the introspective and private chambers of the self, and shutting up the windows of true perception. The consequences of such self-centered love are potentially self-destructive, a fact to which Shakespeare draws our attention in Montague's final ominous words:

> Black and portentous must this humour prove,
> Unless good counsel may the cause remove.

This couplet not only contains the "black and portentous" prophecy of the play's tragic end but a crucial clue that "good counsel" is the necessary component in removing the causes of the portended tragedy. In the event, it is the almost total absence of "good counsel" that leaves Romeo and Juliet at the mercy of their own woeful passions.

Also embedded in these two lines is a significant clue that the feudal or romantic reading of the play is awry. If, as romantic readers of the play maintain, Romeo's love for Rosaline is false whereas his love for Juliet is true, there is nothing "black and portentous" about his "humour" because it will dissipate like the insubstantial thing that it is as soon as Romeo sets eyes on Juliet. Nor is "good counsel" necessary because Romeo's true love for Juliet will exorcise his false love for Rosaline without the need for counsel, good or bad. Montague's final lines are, therefore, worthless from the perspective of a feudal or romantic reading; and yet, to return to Coleridge's insistence that Shakespeare "never introduces a word, or a thought, in vain or out of place", we must surely see these "black and portentous" words as potentially pregnant with meaning. Since the deepest and most portentous meaning of these lines refers to the whole panoramic scope of the play, telescoping us from the opening scene of act 1 to a dark vision of the catastrophic and cataclysmic climax of the final scene of act 5, aren't we forced to consider the possibility that Shakespeare is being censorious about the nature of Romeo's love throughout the whole play, not only about its moping extravagance in the opening scenes? After all, and to return once more to Coleridge, "the smallest fragment of [Shakespeare's] mind not unfrequently gives a clue to a most perfect, regular, and consistent whole." Such a conclusion is reinforced by the fact that the light-shunning metaphor, introduced in relation to Romeo's obsessive love for Rosaline, is maintained throughout the length of the play, especially in relation to Romeo and Juliet's tragic love for each other.

Prior to any further discussion of the play, we should take a step back in order to look at love itself. What is love? And, equally important, what isn't love? Romeo, with the naïve certainty of youth, is confident that he has the answer:

> Love is a smoke rais'd with the fume of sighs;
> Being purg'd, a fire sparkling in lovers' eyes;
> Being vex'd, a sea nourish'd with loving tears.
> What is it else? A madness most discreet,
> A choking gall, and a preserving sweet.
>
> (1.1.188–92)

Love, for Romeo, is a blinding force; it is smoke that gets into the lover's eyes, a bitterness on which he chokes, and a vexatious sea in which he flounders. It is, to put the matter in a nutshell, mere "madness". It is, therefore, no surprise that Romeo confesses that, afflicted with such blindness and madness, he is utterly lost and does not know who he is:

I have lost myself; I am not here:
This is not Romeo, he's some other where.

(1.1.195–96)

In this adolescent discourse on the nature of love, Romeo
will win no prizes for originality. To say that "love is blind"
is, after all, one of the most hackneyed clichés that one can
find. And this appears to be Shakespeare's point. Romeo's
love for Rosaline is not the real thing; it is shallow and
trite. What Romeo calls "love" isn't really love at all, at
least it isn't love in the deeper and deepest sense of the
word. Illustrating this, several critics have shown how
Romeo's words parody the famous love sonnets of Petrarch,
thereby reducing Romeo's declarations of love to the level
of mere cliché.[2] In making Romeo's utterances a thinly disguised pastiche of the celebrated Italian sonneteer, Shakespeare ensures that the young lover's flights of romantic
eloquence plummet toward banality. And this ridicule by
literary association works in both directions, serving to
lampoon the lovelorn lyrics of Petrarch through their mis-
appropriation by the lovestruck teenager. This is made clear
in Mercutio's mocking of Romeo's Petrarchan conceits:

Romeo! humours! madman! passion! lover!
Appear thou in the likeness of a sigh;
Speak but one rhyme and I am satisfied;
Cry but "Ay me!" pronounce but "love" and "dove".

(2.1.8–10)

---

[2] See, for instance, Crystal Downing, "A Rose by Any Other Name: The
Plague of Language in *Romeo and Juliet*", and Rebecca Munroe, "*Romeo and
Juliet* and the Petrarchan Love Poetry Tradition", both published in William
Shakespeare, *Romeo and Juliet*, ed. Joseph Pearce, Ignatius Critical Editions
(San Francisco: Ignatius Press, 2011), pp. 165–81 and 229–44, respectively.

In order to ensure that we make the necessary connection
between Romeo and Petrarch, Mercutio ridicules Romeo's
love for Rosaline by associating it with Petrarch's love for
the unattainable Laura, to whom the Italian's sonnets were
addressed: "Now is he for the numbers that Petrarch flow'd
in; Laura, to his lady, was a kitchen-wench" (2.4.38–39).

Although Shakespeare uses the bawdy irreverence of Mercutio to make the connection between Romeo's unrequited
love for Rosaline and Petrarch's unrequited love for Laura,
we need to avoid the rash conclusion that Mercutio's voice
is that of the playwright. On the contrary, his bawdy "realism" and contempt for Renaissance romance does not enable
him to see or understand Romeo's "love" as coldly or clin-
ically as he and his many critical admirers seem to believe.
Mercutio, as a cynic, is even less capable of true love than
is the lovesick Romeo, and, although he doesn't see it, he is
even more blind to the reality of love than is the besotted
young man he ridicules. He has no time for the numinous
trappings of Petrarchan love and, believing that the numinous is merely nebulous, dismisses the "heavenly" as having its head in the clouds.

Like Romeo, in his earlier pontifications, Mercutio waxes
lyrical about the meaning of "love", most notably in his
Queen Mab speech (1.4.54–95). In Mercutio's eyes "love"
and all such romantic dreams are as "nothing". For Mercutio, the very antithesis of the Petrarchan lover, "love" is
ultimately synonymous with fornication. He sees no distinction between love and lust, the former being a circum-
scribed and euphemistic expression of the latter, and the
latter being merely the honest expression of the former.
When Mercutio dies we don't doubt that he has "known"
women, in the euphemistic sense of the word, but we also
know that he has never truly known women as true lovers

know them, or as husbands know them. We have no trouble believing that Mercutio has lost his virginity, but we suspect that he has never lost his heart. As Romeo says, "He jests at scars that never felt a wound" (2.2.1), a riposte which, though unheard by Mercutio, is as telling in its insightful accuracy as anything Mercutio has uttered from his huge arsenal of punning wit. In speaking of love, Mercutio speaks of something of which he knows nothing. Whereas Romeo's wandering and wayward heart has lost sight of true love, Mercutio's hardened heart has locked love out. One is looking for love in the wrong places; the other refuses to look for it at all. Since, to succumb to a cliché, there are none so blind as those who will not see, Mercutio is more blind to the reality of love than the naïve and lovestruck Romeo. It is not love that is blind but those who are blind to love.

3

JULIET: "TOO SOON MARRED ARE THOSE SO EARLY MADE"

Before we turn our attention to Juliet, the other "star-cross'd lover" at the center of the tragedy, let's pause for a moment in the company of the elusive Rosaline. All that we know of her is learned from the mouths of others. She is the object of Romeo's desire and the subject of Mercutio's scorn. But who is she? The most important clue is given by Romeo in his discussion about her with Benvolio in the play's opening scene, most specifically in his plaintive disdain for her vow of chastity:

> She'll not be hit
> With Cupid's arrow. She hath Dian's wit,
> And in strong proof of chastity well arm'd,
> From Love's weak childish bow she lives unharm'd.
> She will not stay the siege of loving terms,
> Nor bide th' encounter of assailing eyes,
> Nor ope her lap to saint-seducing gold.
> O, she is rich in beauty; only poor
> That, when she dies, with beauty dies her store.
> *Benvolio.* Then she hath sworn that she will still live chaste?
> *Romeo.* She hath, and in that sparing makes huge waste;
> For beauty, starv'd with her severity,
> Cuts beauty off from all posterity.

She is too fair, too wise, wisely too fair,
To merit bliss by making me despair.
She hath forsworn to love, and in that vow
Do I live dead that live to tell it now.

(1.1.206–22)

In these few lines we learn enough about Rosaline to
know that she is not elusively unattainable in the same sense
as Petrarch's Laura. She is not simply, or at any rate she is
not only, a poetic device. She is not a figment of idealized
femininity, a personified abstraction of the ideal of *amour
courtois*. She may remind us of Petrarch's Laura, or by a perverse leap of the imagination of Dante's Beatrice, and no
doubt Shakespeare means her to remind us of these idols of
courtly love, but she is much more than this. She is quite
clearly a woman of flesh and blood who has been forced to
repel Romeo's evidently clumsy and unwelcome advances.
The imagery that Romeo employs is that of warfare, of his
having put her under siege. She resists "the siege of loving
terms" and avoids the "encounter of assailing eyes". And
when the lover's full frontal assault had been repelled, she
shuns the subtle charms of bribery or the promise of worldly
fortune, refusing to open her lap to "saint-seducing gold".
The sexual imagery is entirely appropriate considering that
Romeo's intentions seem to be entirely sexual. He scorns
her desire to remain chaste and treats with dismissive contempt her apparent claim that her vow of chastity is connected to her Christian convictions. She cannot "merit bliss"
by making him despair. She cannot merit heaven by send-
ing him to hell. These words are worth contemplating care-
fully because they offer a key to Romeo's character and to
his notions of "love". He is utterly self-absorbed, desiring
to absorb his lover into his desire for self-gratification.
Whereas true love is desiring the good of the other, Romeo

desires that the other should feel good to him. He doesn't desire that his "love" go to heaven; he doesn't want her to "merit bliss", if it means being refused what he wants. In these lines, Romeo reveals himself as totally self-centered, the epitome of the impetuous adolescent. Indeed, if he weren't so young we would have no hesitation in dubbing him a contemptible cad. This is worth remembering because it is only a matter of hours before he first sets eyes on Juliet. Does Juliet cause a miraculous change in the young man, teaching him how to love truly, as romantic readers of the play believe, or does his residual selfishness and self-absorption contribute to their downfall? Such questions will be addressed presently, but let's tarry a little longer with the beguilingly elusive Rosaline before proceeding to the beautiful and seductive Juliet.

From the paradoxically potent impotence of Romeo's few lines we are introduced to a real woman, albeit a real woman who remains resolutely offstage and therefore apparently unaffected by the tragedy. What can we say of her? Is she, as she claims, a pious young woman, as beautiful interiorly as she is evidently exteriorly? Is she contemplating a religious vocation? Or, perhaps, was the claimed vow of chastity merely a ploy to ward off the unwanted advances of the pestilent suitor? If the former, she represents sanctity, a salvific attribute that is woefully absent, or at least deficient, in the rest of the characters of the play, including the unfortunate Friar. As such, her absence from the stage can be seen as symbolic of the absence of virtue on it.

So much for the paradoxical presence of the absent Rosaline, but what of the all too real and palpitating presence of Juliet?

She is introduced to us, significantly, immediately after the self-absorbed discourse by Romeo that we've just discussed. No sooner has Romeo finished waxing wistful about his failure to seduce Rosaline (at the close of act 1, scene 1) than we learn (in the opening lines of the following scene) of the woman who will take Rosaline's place as the object of his desire. It is also significant that, like Rosaline, we are introduced to Juliet in her absence when Capulet, her father, reminds Paris, her would-be suitor, that she is still a child:

> My child is yet a stranger in the world,
> She hath not seen the change of fourteen years;
> Let two more summers wither in their pride
> Ere we may think her ripe to be a bride.
>
> (1.2.8–11)

When Paris replies that "younger than she are happy mothers made" (1.2.12), Capulet's response is cutting: "And too soon marr'd are those so early made" (1.2.13).

To put the matter bluntly and frankly, Shakespeare makes it plain that Juliet is still a child, only thirteen years old, barely a teenager. This singularly crucial fact is all too often overlooked by modern critics who bestow upon her an adulthood she does not possess. The tenderness of her years and its importance to a true understanding of the play were discussed with eloquence by John Quincy Adams, in the days when U.S. presidents possessed an understanding of culture, in a letter to the Shakespearean actor James Henry Hackett:

> The age of Juliet seems to be the key to her character throughout the play, an essential ingredient in the intense sympathy which she inspires; and Shakespeare has marked it, not only in her discourse, but even in her name, the diminutive of tender affections applied only to childhood.

If Shakespeare had exhibited upon the stage a woman of nineteen, he would have dismissed her nurse and called her Julia. She might still have been a very interesting character, but the whole color and complexion of the play must have been changed. An intelligent, virtuous woman, in love with a youth of assorted age and congenial character, is always a person of deep interest in the drama. But that interest is heightened and redoubled when, to the sympathy with the lover, you add all the kind affections with which you share in the joys and sorrows of the child. There is childishness in the discourse of Juliet, and the poet has shown us why; because she had scarcely ceased to be a child.[1]

The fact that Shakespeare is intent on stressing Juliet's immaturity is apparent in his making Juliet two years younger than her age in his source. In Brooke's *Tragicall Historye of Romeus and Juliet* she is almost sixteen, and in another English version of the tragedy that Shakespeare may have known, the translation of a novella by Matteo Bandello, she is almost eighteen. It is also noteworthy that in both these earlier versions the older Juliets were still considered too young to marry. And yet Shakespeare makes her even younger. He wants us to see Juliet as a child who is thrown prematurely into an adult world in which she not only loses her innocence but her life. This is the heart of the tragedy.

Countering such a reading of the play, romantics will no doubt stress that the youth of the lovers is merely a device to highlight the unblemished purity of their true love. At the other extreme, cynical readers, taking their cue from Mercutio, will doubtless suggest that Shakespeare makes Juliet

---

[1] John Quincy Adams, Letter to James Henry Hackett, November 4, 1845; reprinted in Hackett's *Notes, Criticisms and Correspondence upon Shakespeare's Plays and Actors* (New York: Carleton, 1863), 222–23.

so young merely to show his male audience that Romeo is courting a true virgin. These two objections can be dismissed by closely scrutinizing the times in which Shakespeare was living and the moral and social conventions that prevailed in late Elizabethan England. Many social historians believe that children reached physical maturity, or puberty, later in sixteenth-century England than they do today. It is believed that girls matured at fourteen to fifteen, and boys at around sixteen.[2] As such, Juliet would have seemed even more of a child to Shakespeare's audience than she does to today's audiences. Youths under fifteen were still considered children, and early teenage marriages were rare indeed. Figures showing the age at first marriage during the period in which Shakespeare was writing indicate that only 6 percent of marriages were at the age of fifteen, and no figures are given for marriages below that age. Juliet was not yet fourteen when the action of the play takes place.[3] In the few cases on record in which children were married, they were not permitted to consummate their vows until much older.

Popular manuals of health in sixteenth-century England cautioned against the permanent damage to a young woman's health that could be caused by early marriage and its consummation, and by the early pregnancies that were its consequence. The grandmother of Anne Clopton, a contemporary

[2] Lawrence Stone, *The Family, Sex and Marriage in England, 1500–1800* (New York: Harper, 1977), p. 512; Barbara Everett, *Young Hamlet: Essays on Shakespeare's Tragedies* (Oxford: Clarendon, 1989), p. 116; Ann Jennalie Cook, *Making a Match: Courtship in Shakespeare and His Society* (Princeton: Princeton University Press, 1991), pp. 17, 20; J. Karl Franson, "'Too Soon Marr'd': Juliet's Age as Symbol in *Romeo and Juliet*", in *Papers on Language and Literature* 32, no. 3 (1996).

[3] Lawrence Stone, *The Crisis of the Aristocracy, 1558–1641* (Oxford: Clarendon, 1965), p. 654.

of Shakespeare, opposed the proposed marriage of her thirteen-year-old granddaughter on the grounds of the "danger [that] might ensue to her very life from her extreme youth".[4] Such parental concern reflects Capulet's riposte to Paris that "too soon marr'd are those so early made". Shakespeare's own daughter Susanna was herself around Juliet's age when he was writing the play. As the father of a twelve-year-old daughter, Shakespeare's perspective is that of a parent.

The consensus in Elizabethan England was that marriage before sixteen was dangerous.[5] In consequence, eighteen was considered the earliest reasonable age for motherhood, and the ideal ages for men and women to marry were considered to be thirty and twenty, respectively.[6] Elizabethan women married, on average, in their early to mid-twenties, and men, on average, a few years later.[7] According to the historian Peter Laslett, who examined a thousand marriage licenses from the years immediately after Shakespeare wrote *Romeo and Juliet*, "the average age of ... Elizabethan and Jacobean brides was something like 24 and the average of bridegrooms was nearly 28".[8] The historian Christopher Hill noted that this is the oldest of any society known in

---

[4] Ibid., p. 656.

[5] Ibid., pp. 656–57.

[6] Caroll Camden, *The Elizabethan Woman* (Mamaroneck, N.Y.: Appel, 1995), p. 94; Cook, *Making a Match*, p. 23.

[7] Peter Laslett, *The World We Have Lost: English Society before the Coming of Industry* (New York: Scribner's, 1965), pp. 81–86; Stone, *Family, Sex and Marriage*, pp. 49, 490; Cook, *Making a Match*, pp. 265–67. The aristocracy married, on average, a little younger, due to arranged marriages designed to secure an heiress or to seal a political alliance, but even among the aristocracy the average spousal age at marriage at the time Shakespeare wrote *Romeo and Juliet* was twenty-one or twenty-two years of age.

[8] Laslett, *World We Have Lost*, p. 82.

history.[9] Shakespeare's own wife and his daughter Susanna conformed to the norms of Elizabethan society, marrying at about twenty-six and twenty-four, respectively, while his younger daughter, Judith, did not marry until she was thirty-one.

The literary critic J. Karl Franson concludes from this contextual evidence that Shakespeare's audience would have been shocked at Juliet's age and the way in which the child was propelled, unprepared, into an adult world with which she was ill-equipped to cope: "That Capulet would offer his daughter to Paris despite her 'extreme youth' . . . must have been appalling to an Elizabethan." Franson also conjectured whether Shakespeare's "own unsatisfactory marriage at eighteen may have initiated him to some of the unpleasant consequences of premature marriage".[10] In similar vein, Laslett concluded, not unreasonably, that Shakespeare's *Romeo and Juliet* might have been written specifically as a cautionary tale about the dangers of erotic love and premature marriage among boys and girls.[11] The literary critic Maureen Johnson argued that Shakespeare considered Romeo and Juliet "sonnet lovers", a couple devoted to Venus and the religion of love.[12] Significantly, the age of love, when one is dominated by Venus (the power of erotic love), was thought to begin at fourteen, connecting the lover symbolically and symbiotically to the sonnet itself. And this brings us back to Shakespeare's apparent dialectic with Petrarchan "love".

[9] Christopher Hill, *The Collected Essays of Christopher Hill*, vol. 3, *People and Ideas in 17th Century England* (Brighton, England: Harvester, 1986), p. 195.

[10] Franson, " 'Too soon marr'd' ".

[11] Laslett, *World We Have Lost*, p. 84.

[12] Maureen Johnson, *"What's in a Name?": Astrology and Onomastics in "Romeo and Juliet"* (Ann Arbor, Mich.: UMI, 1983), p. 128.

Following Sir Thomas Wyatt's popularization of Petrarch earlier in the century, the sonnet became almost ubiquitous in Elizabethan England, so much so that around twelve hundred English sonnets "have survived in print" from the 1590s alone.[13] As such, and as Crystal Downing observes, Shakespeare wrote *Romeo and Juliet* "at the height of the 1590s sonnet fad".[14] It is surely significant, therefore, that the first conversation between Romeo and Juliet takes the form of a sonnet in which the lines are shared by the two "sonnet lovers", culminating in a kiss (of which we shall say more in the next chapter).

J. Karl Franson ends his essay on the symbolism attached to Juliet's age with the following sobering conclusion:

> Shakespeare symbolizes Juliet's youth in a display of numerological virtuosity designed to impress upon his audience and readers her unripeness for adulthood and its attendant complexities. Through a counting of letters, words, lines, stage entrances, and hours, he transforms her age into a force that drives the play to its catastrophe. Attention to her premature introduction to adulthood, in turn, shifts much of the blame for the disaster to the Capulets, Paris, the Nurse, the Friar, adults who pressure and manipulate Juliet while she is still a child. The care with which Shakespeare encodes Juliet's age into the text leads us to believe his imagination was captured by her as by no other character in the play.[15]

[13] Hallett Smith, "Sonnets", *The Riverside Shakespeare*, ed. G. Blakemore Evans (Boston: Houghton Mifflin, 1974), p. 1746.

[14] Crystal Downing, "A Rose by Any Other Name: The Plague of Language in *Romeo and Juliet*", in William Shakespeare, *Romeo and Juliet*, ed. Joseph Pearce, Ignatius Critical Editions (San Francisco: Ignatius Press, 2011), p. 166.

[15] Franson, "'Too Soon Marr'd'".

Franson's chief sin of omission is his leaving Romeo off the list of those to blame for Juliet's downfall. Romeo is not blameless in his relationship with Juliet, a fact that Shakespeare seems to suggest by making him considerably older than she. It is, for instance, interesting that he makes Juliet younger than she is in the source poem, whereas he makes Romeo apparently older. He shaves two years off Juliet's age, accentuating her childishness, but appears to add at least two years to the age of her lover. Brooke describes Romeo as so young that his chin sports no beard,[16] thereby conveying Romeo as a mere boy, but Shakespeare clearly suggests that he is older. Although the Nurse describes him as "young Romeo" (2.4.116) it should be remembered that even a twenty-year-old would be considered "young" to the much older Nurse.

His one sin of omission notwithstanding, Franson's overall conclusion is resoundingly and perceptively incisive. Juliet was "too soon marr'd" by the neglect or manipulation of callous and heartless adults. At the play's tragic heart is the broken heart of a child.

---

[16] "One Romeus, who was of race a Montague,/Upon whose tender chin, as yet, no manlike beard there grew." Arthur Brooke, *The Tragicall Historye of Romeus and Juliet* (1562, lines 55–56); reprinted in Geoffrey Bullough, ed., *Narrative and Dramatic Sources of Shakespeare*, vol. 1 (London: Routledge, 1957).

4

VENUS AND THE VIRGIN

When the devout religion of mine eye
Maintains such falsehood, then turn tears to fires;
And these, who, often drown'd, could never die,
Transparent heretics, be burnt for liars!
One fairer than my love! The all-seeing sun
Ne'er saw her match since first the world begun.

(1.2.88–93)

These lines, so suggestive of Romeo's later eulogizing of Juliet,
are uttered in praise of Rosaline. Within a few hours of these
words being spoken, Romeo will forget the "devout religion" of his eye, proving that his eyes were indeed "transparent heretics" worshipping a false goddess. Clearly Shakespeare
is mocking the besotted lover by placing such Petrarchan platitudes on his lips, heightening the hyperbole to the level of
hilarity. There is, however, a serious theological dimension
implicit in the religious symbolism. Here we see Romeo as a
"sonnet lover", devoted to Venus and the religion of erotic
love. From a Christian perspective, Romeo's love is idolatry,
the worshipping of false gods, or, to be precise, goddesses.
There is none fairer than his love, the idol of his eye's "devout
religion", not in the whole world, nor in the whole history
of the world, as the omniscient sun would testify.

Romeo's faith in false gods is fickle, as can be seen from his words upon first setting eyes on Juliet:

> O, she doth teach the torches to burn bright!
> It seems she hangs upon the cheek of night
> As a rich jewel in an Ethiop's ear—
> Beauty too rich for use, for earth too dear!
> So shows a snowy dove trooping with crows
> As yonder lady o'er her fellows shows.
> The measure done, I'll watch her place of stand,
> And, touching hers, make blessed my rude hand.
> Did my heart love till now? Forswear it, sight;
> For I ne'er saw true beauty till this night.
>
> $$(1.5.42-51)$$

From his insistence with religious fervor, a few hours earlier, that even the "all-seeing sun" had never seen a woman fairer than his Rosaline since the dawn of time, Romeo now ranks Rosaline amongst the crows in comparison with the "snowy dove" that he espies across the room. Forsaking and forswearing his former lover, he is now, at an instant, in love with a woman whose name he does not even know. For romantic readers of the play, following their hearts and forsaking and forswearing their heads, this "love at first sight" is one of the most beautiful things in the play. It is as pure and passionate as it is impetuous and impulsive. It is truly momentous, in the sense that it surrenders itself to the moment, and will not be assuaged by reason, temperance, or prudence. There can be no brakes on such a love as it hurls itself heedlessly into the arms of the beloved, a headless heart hurtling toward a breathlessly exhilarating consummation.

Shakespeare, who invariably and unerringly perceives the human condition with the incisive insight of his genius, understands the exhilaration of the sort of love that Venus offers and which Romeo desires. Indeed, from this moment onwards, the whole action of the play accelerates. It is noteworthy, for instance, that Shakespeare condenses the whole drama into five breathless days, whereas in the poem, which is his source, the action takes place over several months. The question is not whether Shakespeare understands such romantic passion; it is what he has to say about it.

We don't have to wait long. A few lines later, after a brief interregnum in which an exchange between Tybalt and Capulet reminds us of the perilous territory into which the lover is about to stray, Romeo approaches Juliet. He is as forward and forthright in his amorous advances as he had been with Rosaline, taking Juliet's hand before he has even spoken a word to her. This time, however, he finds the object of his desire receptive to his charms. The maiden does not withdraw her hand from his, and, finding no drawbridge of chastity being raised to repel his advances, he raises the ante, moving from the touch of hands to the touch of lips:

> If I profane with my unworthiest hand
> This holy shrine, the gentle sin is this:
> My lips, two blushing pilgrims, ready stand
> To smooth that rough touch with a tender kiss.
>
> (1.5.91–94)

The rest of their exchange, which forms, up to the first kiss, one of the most wonderful sonnets ever to grace the English language, warrants our close attention:

> *Juliet.* Good pilgrim, you do wrong your hand too much,
> Which mannerly devotion shows in this;
> For saints have hands that pilgrims' hands do touch,
> And palm to palm is holy palmers' kiss.

Romeo. Have not saints lips, and holy palmers too?
Juliet. Ay, pilgrim, lips that they must use in pray'r.
Romeo. O, then, dear saint, let lips do what hands do!
   They pray; grant thou, lest faith turn to despair.
Juliet. Saints do not move, though grant for prayers' sake.
Romeo. Then move not while my prayer's effect I take.
   Thus from my lips, by thine, my sin is purg'd.
                                    [*Kissing her.*]
Juliet. Then have my lips the sin that they have took.
Romeo. Sin from my lips? O trespass sweetly urg'd!
   Give me my sin again.   ⌊*Kissing her.*⌋
                                    (1.5.95–108)

Whereas Romeo's opening lines, forming the first quatrain of the sonnet, had been seductively suggestive and sexually charged, Juliet's response, forming the second quatrain, baptizes Romeo's words with a Christian metaphor, reminding him that the hands of saints and pilgrims kiss, i.e., touch, in prayer.

Romeo's libido is not to be deflected or deflated by his quarry's conventional piety. "Have not saints lips," he asks, "and holy palmers too?" Again he is rebutted with the gentle rejoinder that their lips, like their hands, must be used in prayer. Faced with this second defensive parry, Romeo's response becomes more impassioned, perhaps even strained with a hint of desperation:

   O then, dear saint, let lips do what hands do.
   They pray; grant thou, lest faith turn to despair.

With his customary hyperbolic abuse of religious imagery, he has already canonized the girl, assured of her virtue even before he is sure of her name. Furthermore, his hint that his faith might turn to despair if his suit is not granted reminds us uncomfortably of his earlier complaint that the chaste Rosaline could not "merit bliss" by making him despair.

It is likely, at this point, that one final and firm riposte from his new love would elicit the same plaintive response from the desperate lover. Unlike Rosaline, however, Juliet is clearly attracted by Romeo's charms and is torn between chaste decorum and erotic desire. As the mysterious stranger manipulates her words to serve his amorous purposes, bestowing the first kiss, the girl's struggle with her conscience is strained to the limit. This kiss, almost certainly Juliet's first, is a new and strange experience, throwing her into confusion. Her conflicted emotions are aroused still further by another of Romeo's inappropriate religious images: "Thus from my lips, by thine, my sin is purg'd." The metaphor of the "sinful kiss" is taken literally by the naïve Juliet, causing her to exclaim in alarm that she has indeed shared in a sinful act in permitting herself to be kissed by the stranger: "Then have my lips the sin that they have took." Her sense of sin is no doubt heightened by the erotic pleasure it had given her. Romeo, seizing the opportunity, manipulates her words once again to steal a second kiss: "Sin from my lips? O trespass sweetly urg'd! / Give me my sin again."

Although romantic readers of this scene invariably bestow maturity on the thirteen-year-old, enabling her to play her part in the intertwined sonnet with a suave savoir faire belying her age, Shakespeare's use of the "sin" metaphor suggests a clear moral dimension to the exchange. The kiss does not merely transmit the sin metaphorically; it does so literally. The erotically charged Romeo has inflamed desire in the object of his advances, succeeding with Juliet where he had failed with the presumably more mature Rosaline. And let's remind ourselves once again of Juliet's age. She is thirteen, not yet fourteen. Since Shakespeare deliberately sets his play two weeks before Juliet's fourteenth birthday, he is making it abundantly clear that she is still a child. As such, it is hard to concur with Harley Granville-Barker's suggestion that there is "something sacramental, something shy, grave and sweet" [1] about the lovers' first exchange. On the contrary, Romeo's imagery in this first encounter is profane even when it masquerades as religious, whereas Juliet's religious imagery is charmingly and disarmingly genuine. Juliet might be considered "shy, grave and sweet", but this can hardly be applied to Romeo's manipulative advances. On the contrary, his fickleness with regard to Rosaline leads us to suspect a venality in his character and a venereal motive in his actions, reminding ourselves that "venereal" comes from the Latin *venereus*, i.e., that which belongs to Venus. Venus has no time for virgins, nor has her young disciple. As for the sonnet and the brief addendum that follows it, which constitutes the first exchange, it can be seen as a masterful intertwining of the sacred (Juliet) and the profane (Romeo). It is a sweet-and-sour mixture of the sacred and sacrilegious, culminating in a sexually transmitted sin, but it is not, *pace* Granville-Barker, "something sacramental".

The foregoing nonromantic reading of the lovers' first exchange seems to be vindicated by the words of the Chorus immediately after the scene we've just discussed:

Now old desire doth in his death-bed lie,
And young affection gapes to be his heir;
That fair for which love groan'd for and would die,
With tender Juliet match'd, is now not fair.
Now Romeo is belov'd and loves again,
Alike bewitched by the charm of looks.

(2, prol. 1–6)

---

[1] Harley Granville-Barker, *Romeo and Juliet* (London: Nick Hern Books, 1993), p. 36.

The voice of the Chorus, being impartial and aloof, and therefore closest to the narrative voice of the playwright, makes no distinction between the nature of Romeo's love for Rosaline and that which he has for Juliet. The "old desire" for Rosaline may be dead, but the "young affection" for Juliet desires eagerly to be "his heir". One "love" has simply been replaced by another in its likeness. Romeo is "belov'd and loves again, / Alike bewitched by the charm of looks". Again, no distinction is made between the earlier love and its heir. Indeed, the Chorus seems to be suggesting that there *is* no distinction. Romeo simply "loves again". He has not spurned false love for true, but merely loves both women in the same way. In this sense the phrase "alike bewitched" seems to have a double meaning. Romeo and Juliet are "alike bewitched", i.e., bewitched by each other, but Romeo is also "alike bewitched" in that he was bewitched by Rosaline and Juliet alike. In both cases, he is bewitched by physical beauty, by "the charm of looks". And let's not forget that the love between Romeo and Juliet is skin-deep and purely physical at this stage. Romeo and Juliet do not know each other. They do not even know each other's names. Romeo declares his "love" before he has even spoken a single word to his beloved. How can such love be anything but superficial, a bewitchment of the eye in response to great physical beauty? This, at any rate, seems to be the question that Shakespeare, via the Chorus, is asking.

The question is asked again, immediately, by Mercutio, in his savage lampooning of Petrarchan love,[2] and in his disdain for the "gossip Venus" and for Cupid, "her purblind son", the latter of whom he regards as a swindler and

---

[2] 2.1.7–10. See the discussion about Shakespeare's satire on Petrarchan love on pages 27–28 above.

confidence trickster.[3] Mercutio sees Romeo as a victim of Venus, struck by Cupid's duplicitous dart, and, as such, is struck witless by love: "Romeo! humours! madman! passion! lover!" (2.1.7). For Mercutio, "Romeo", "madman", and "lover" are synonyms. Responding to Mercutio's jesting, the sober-minded Benvolio observes that Romeo is not so much a madman as a blind man who is at home in the darkness of his passions: "Blind is his love, and best befits the dark" (2.1.32).

And so, with Mercutio's description of Romeo's madness and Benvolio's lament at his blindness, and with the Chorus' suggestion that the young lover is still bewitched by the same enchantment that had overpowered him in the presence of Rosaline, we are prepared by Shakespeare for the following scene in which his besotted lovers meet once again.

---

[3] 2.1.11–13. Mercutio's description of Venus' partially blind son as "Young Abraham Cupid" is an allusion to an "Abraham man", one of a class of beggars, thrown into poverty by the dissolution of the monasteries, who wandered the countryside feigning illness to obtain alms, i.e., Cupid is a beggarly con-man.

5

FALLING FROM THE BALCONY

But, soft! What light through yonder window breaks?
It is the east, and Juliet is the sun.
Arise, fair sun, and kill the envious moon,
Who is already sick and pale with grief
That thou her maid art far more fair than she.
Be not her maid since she is envious;
Her vestal livery is but sick and green,
And none but fools do wear it; cast it off.

(2.2.2–9)

Romeo's opening lines in the famous balcony scene are so familiar that we are swept away by the anticipation of what follows without lingering long enough to engage their meaning. Juliet is the sun, the light by which Romeo sees (eclipsing all other perspectives), who is in conflict with the "envious" moon, equated with Diana, the goddess of chastity. Juliet is not only "more fair" than the goddess and therefore a worthy object of his idolatry; Romeo wishes her to "kill" the goddess of chastity and cast off her robes of virginity, her "vestal livery", which "none but fools do wear". In describing Juliet's livery as "vestal", Romeo invokes another goddess, Vesta, to whom the vestal virgins consecrated their virginity, taking a vow of chastity. In the

Christian culture in which Shakespeare was writing, the adjective "vestal" was applied to any woman of spotless chastity, especially one who consecrates her life to religion, such as a nun. In stating that only fools live chastely, Romeo is reiterating the disdain for chastity that he showed in his lament over Rosaline's rejection of his amorous advances, and in hoping that Juliet will "kill" chastity and "cast it [her virginity] off", he hopes that she will do what Rosaline resolutely refused to do. In this sense, Juliet is an anti-Rosaline, one who succumbs to seduction and faces the consequences.

In contrast to Romeo's carnality and his reduction of religion and myth to mere metaphor, Juliet's opening lines in the balcony scene are pregnant with the deepest realist philosophy.[1] After asking one of the most famous questions in all of literature ("O Romeo, Romeo! wherefore art thou Romeo?" [2.2.33]), Juliet muses over the meaning of names:

> 'Tis but thy name that is my enemy;
> Thou art thyself, though not a Montague.
> What's Montague? It is nor hand, nor foot,

[1] Christian philosophy is rooted in realism, the assertion that universals have real existence, as opposed to the opposite view of nominalism, the assertion that universals have no real existence but are merely names. The former view, embraced by Christian orthodoxy, was held by Socrates, Plato, and Aristotle, and was affirmed by the great Christian philosophers, such as Augustine and Thomas Aquinas; the latter view was held by William of Ockham and would later be championed by Thomas Hobbes. Shakespeare was clearly aware of the philosophical controversy between realism and nominalism that had been raging for almost three hundred years by the time that *Romeo and Juliet* was written. As an orthodox Christian, Shakespeare defended the realist position, particularly in plays such as *Hamlet*, *The Merchant of Venice*, and *Macbeth*, whereas the nominalist position, which he condemned, became the source of much of the relativism that was growing in influence in Elizabethan England.

Nor arm, nor face, nor any other part
Belonging to a man. O, be some other name!
What's in a name? That which we call a rose
By any other name would smell as sweet;
So Romeo would, were he not Romeo call'd,
Retain that dear perfection which he owes
Without that title. Romeo, doff thy name;
And for thy name, which is no part of thee,
Take all myself.

(2.2.38–48)

Again, we are tempted to allow ourselves to be swept away by the beauty of the lines without pausing to ponder their deepest meaning, a temptation that must be resisted because Shakespeare imbues Juliet's words with metaphysical profundity. She is differentiating between Romeo's *essential* being, his human individuality, and that which is only his as an *accidental* quality, the name he inherited from his parents. Romeo is not defined by his name, the label that convention has placed upon him, but by his personhood, that which is *essentially* his regardless of convention. This is not merely academic or esoteric, but delineates the difference between Christian realism and its nominalist antithesis, the latter of which informs modern manifestations of relativism, such as postmodernism and deconstructionism. As such, Juliet's words remind us of the realist philosophy underpinning Bassanio's pondering of the meaning of the three caskets in *The Merchant of Venice*, and also Hamlet's preoccupation with the difference between that which is and that which only seems to be.

Shakespeare uses the philosophical digressions of Juliet, Bassanio, and Hamlet to discuss those fundamental issues of metaphysics that had been dividing philosophers since the advent of the nominalism of William of Ockham almost three hundred years earlier. The fact that Shakespeare, through the voices of Juliet, Bassanio, and Hamlet, invariably comes down on the side of the *realism* of Plato, Aristotle, and Thomas Aquinas and against the *nominalism* of Ockham and its protorelativism is further evidence of the Bard's Christian orthodoxy. According to the realists, the *essence* or *being*[2] of a thing is immutable and is contrasted with those attributes of a thing that are changeable or *accidental*, or, to employ Bassanio's phrase, merely *ornamental*.[3] To the postphilosophical culture in which we find ourselves, such distinctions might themselves seem irrelevant or merely ornamental, but to Shakespeare and the culture of sixteenth-century Europe, such issues were at the center of the cauldron of controversy and conflict that had been bubbling since the Renaissance and had been boiling over since the Reformation.[4] For Shakespeare and his contemporaries, the battle between realism and nominalism was a very hot topic, and Shakespeare clearly takes a position in defense of the former against the latter.

Such is the woeful state of much modern criticism and its concomitant philosophical ignorance that Juliet's words are actually considered by many critics to be nominalist when they are in fact a rebuttal of nominalism. Nominalists believe that certain types of things (universals) have no existence beyond the name that is given to them; Juliet is obviously

---

[2] *Esse*, from which "essence" and "essential" are derived, is the verb "to be" in Latin.

[3] *The Merchant of Venice*, 3.2.97–98. All quotes from that play are taken from William Shakespeare, *The Merchant of Venice*, ed. Joseph Pearce, Ignatius Critical Editions (San Francisco: Ignatius Press, 2009).

[4] Nominalism soon after found powerful champions in the philosophical writings of Francis Bacon (1561–1626), Thomas Hobbes (1588–1679), and René Descartes (1596–1650). Shakespeare's own position is clearly inimical to that professed by these pioneers of modern philosophy.

saying the opposite, i.e., that Romeo exists regardless of the name that we give to him. This crucial difference was discussed with eloquence by the literary critic Richard Harp:

> Juliet has often been accused of the philosophical error of nominalism, the view that universal concepts such as honor or virtue exist in name only and not in reality. The content with which we invest such concepts, so the argument goes, is dependent on subjective opinion or preference. There is no space here for a formal refutation of the nominalist position; let us say only that Juliet is not a nominalist.... [S]he is not denying that there is such a person as Romeo when she invites him to "refuse [his] name"—how could she when she has just been smitten by him?—any more than she is denying that there is such a thing as a rose when she famously says, "[A] rose / By any other name would smell as sweet" (2.2.43– 44). She is clearly right—the world's languages have all manner of different words for that same rose. And she is certainly not saying that a real rose is only a word; rather, she is saying that no word, ultimately, can be adequate to the thing that is a rose—a very different matter. Her love for Romeo is of the same kind, as evidenced by what she says to him when she comes to Friar Lawrence's cell to be wed: "[M]y true love is grown to such excess / I cannot sum up ... half my wealth" (2.6.33–34). As there are graces beyond the reach of art, so there are things beyond the reach of words.[5]

Before we leave this important philosophical digression and return to the two lovers, we need hardly remind ourselves that Juliet's words do not mean that she thinks explicitly in the technical philosophical terms that we have employed

[5] Richard Harp, "Why Juliet Makes the Torches to Burn Bright: The Luminous Quality of Beauty", in William Shakespeare, *Romeo and Juliet*, ed. Joseph Pearce, Ignatius Critical Editions (San Francisco: Ignatius Press, 2011), pp. 187–88.

to explain them. She asks a simple question ("O Romeo, Romeo! wherefore art thou Romeo?" [2.2.33]) and muses on it with wistful perception, much as Hamlet ponders the question "to be or not to be" (3.1.56)[6] at the beginning of his famous soliloquy. Her innocent common sense comes to the same conclusion as the realist philosophers: *a rose by any other word would smell as sweet.* Neither Romeo nor the rose is defined by the names that we give them but by who or what they truly are. One does not need to be a philosopher to be a realist.

The solid substance of reality, as opposed to the slippery elusiveness of words, is also evident in Juliet's use of the word "owe":

> What's in a name? That which we call a rose
> By any other word would smell as sweet;
> So Romeo would, were he not Romeo call'd,
> Retain that dear perfection which he owes
> Without that title.
>
> (2.2.43–47)

In modern editions of the play, the word "owes" is almost invariably glossed as "owns", even though there is every reason to suspect that Shakespeare intends it to mean the former and not the latter, or, to be precise, that he is using the word in such a way that "owes" and "owns" are conflated and subsumed within each other. Both words have the same root in Old High German, *eigan*, from which we also get the word "ought".[7] This is hugely significant. Romeo

---

[6] All quotes from *Hamlet* are taken from William Shakespeare, *Hamlet*, ed. Joseph Pearce, Ignatius Critical Editions (San Francisco: Ignatius Press, 2008).

[7] The connection between "own", "owe", and "ought" has important ramifications in the fields of political philosophy and economics, connecting ownership inextricably with the moral obligations that accompany it. This

does not *own* his "dear perfection"; he *owes* it to God, who bestowed it upon him, and, therefore, he *ought* to use the gifts given him by grace, the source of all that is dear and perfect in him, to honor God through the living of a virtuous life. A life of virtue is what we *owe* to God for the life and "dear perfection" he has given us. Man does not *own* his life; he *owes* it to the One who gave it to him. Shakespeare, as a Christian playwright communicating with an overwhelmingly Christian audience, has an understanding of life in which man is indebted to his Creator. If we forget this, and interpret the play in the light of an anthropocentric conception of reality in which we *own* our lives and destinies as a manmade right, we will fail to understand the meaning of Shakespeare's plays.

After Romeo reveals himself, Juliet is fearful of the danger in which he has placed himself by trespassing on the property of his family's enemies, exclaiming that "if they do see thee, they will murder thee" (2.2.70). Romeo's reply is brazenly defiant but also portentously prophetic: "Alack, there lies more peril in thine eye / Than twenty of their swords" (2.2.71–72). Juliet, by contrast, is far from brazen, confessing her embarrassment at being overheard by the concealed Romeo:

> Thou knowest the mask of night is on my face,
> Else would a maiden blush bepaint my cheek
> For that which thou hast heard me speak tonight.
> (2.2.85–87)

Knowing that Romeo has overheard her words, she can scarcely deny that she loves him, but she remains uneasy at

---

understanding is at the core of the Catholic Church's teaching on subsidiarity but is almost entirely absent in conventional economics and especially in its laissez-faire manifestations.

the position in which his eavesdropping has placed her. The rest of her speech is a charming oscillation between candid expressions of love and bashful protestations at the indecorous predicament in which she finds herself because of his trespassing on her private thoughts.

> Fain would I dwell on form; fain, fain deny
> What I have spoke; but farewell compliment!
> Dost thou love me? I know thou wilt say ay,
> And I will take thy word; yet, if thou swear'st,
> Thou mayst prove false; at lovers' perjuries
> They say Jove laughs. O gentle Romeo,
> If thou dost love, pronounce it faithfully.
> Or, if thou think'st I am too quickly won,
> I'll frown, and be perverse, and say thee nay,
> So thou wilt woo; but else, not for the world.
> In truth, fair Montague, I am too fond;
> And therefore thou mayst think my haviour light;
> But trust me, gentleman, I'll prove more true
> Than those that have more cunning to be strange.
> I should have been more strange, I must confess,
> But that thou overheard'st, ere I was ware,
> My true love's passion. Therefore pardon me,
> And not impute this yielding to light love,
> Which the dark night hath so discovered.
>
> (2.2.88–106)

The whole scenario of young love is virgin territory for her, and she betrays a confused naïveté. What should a virtuous girl do in such circumstances? She protests that she would have preferred to have been courted with the customary propriety ("Fain would I dwell on form") and that it would have been better if Romeo had never heard her private thoughts ("fain, fain deny / What I have spoke"), but, his having overheard her lover's soliloquy, it's too late for such propriety ("But farewell compliment"). The phrase "fain would I" means "I would be glad to", and since the root of the word "fain" is the Old High German *gifehan*, which means "rejoice", the word "glad" is, if anything, an understatement of her feelings. She seems to wish in all earnest that Romeo had not heard her earlier words so that he might woo her in the customary manner. Since, however, it seems to be too late for such etiquette she asks him candidly whether he loves her. Are her feelings reciprocated? She's not sure and craves reassurance. Yet almost immediately she retreats into the embarrassment of her situation. Has she been too forward? Has she said too much? Has she been immodest? Does she sound like a woman of easy virtue?

> Or, if thou think'st I am too quickly won,
> I'll frown, and be perverse, and say thee nay,
> So thou wilt woo.

She is concerned that her candor might lead Romeo to believe her behavior "light", i.e., immodest or unchaste, but promises him that she will be more true than those who feign reluctance or shyness when being wooed by a lover. She ends, as she began, with a bashful reiteration of her desire that Romeo had not overheard her words and with concern that his hearing them might have led him to believe she was an unchaste or frivolous woman:

> I should have been more strange, I must confess,
> But that thou overheard'st ere I was ware,
> My true-love's passion. Therefore pardon me,
> And not impute this yielding to light love,
> Which the dark night hath so discovered.

Juliet's confused innocence is charming, winning us over. Yet it is also alarming, leading us to fear for her future. She is straying into uncharted and treacherous territory.

Needless to say, Romeo is not in the least concerned that Juliet might have been too forward or that she might have lacked chastity. He seems to make a habit of being too forward and clearly spurns the very thought of chastity. His response to her charmingly disarming words is the regurgitation of Petrarchan platitudes and clichés:

> Lady, by yonder blessed moon I vow,
> That tips with silver all these fruit-tree tops.
> (2.2.107–8)

Shakespeare seems to accentuate the banality of Romeo's words, not simply through his descent into cliché but also through Romeo's contradictory use of the lunar metaphor. Moments earlier he had spurned the moon as "envious" and "sick and pale", and the moon's livery as "sick and green", desiring that Juliet should "cast it off". Now the moon is "blessed", and the young lover is eager to swear by it. It is he, not Juliet, who is frivolous and unchaste, and, if the lunar metaphor is still intended as an allegory of Diana, the goddess of chastity, he is also a hypocrite and a liar. Having heard Juliet's concern that she might appear unchaste, he swears by the moon, making his own hypocritical and disingenuous vow of chastity in spite of his earlier declaration that "none but fools" make such vows. In the light of such lunacy, it is hard to avoid the symbolism inherent in Shakespeare's introduction of the fruit trees at this precise moment. In the very throes of his hypocrisy and deception, Romeo draws Juliet's attention to a fruit tree. He is a seducer in a garden, tempting his lover to pluck the forbidden fruit. He is below, desirous of bringing his beloved

down to his level. Juliet, still aloft if not sufficiently aloof in
the balcony above, is as yet unfallen but is in grave peril of
falling. The prelapsarian symbolism is inescapable. As with
the first kiss at the Capulets' ball, the lovers' second meeting in the garden is all about sin.

Juliet's candor has no time for Romeo's cant, echoing
our own impatience with his banality, and she cuts him
short. She does not want him to swear by the "inconstant
moon", lest Romeo's own love "prove likewise variable"
(2.2.108, 111). For once, Romeo is left dumbstruck. If not
the moon, what shall he swear by? It is now that Juliet
appears to fall definitively:

> Do not swear at all;
> Or, if thou wilt, swear by thy gracious self,
> Which is the god of my idolatry,
> And I'll believe thee.
>
> (2.2.113–14)

From this point on, the action accelerates, not merely in
the sense that Shakespeare conflates his plot into a few freneti-
cally breathless days, but also in the sense that Juliet joins
her lover in the reckless abandonment of all temperance,
prudence, and decorum. She has a new god to worship and
will follow him into the abyss.

Having confessed her faith in Romeo as the god of her
idolatry, Juliet utters one final and ultimately futile prot-
estation at their lack of temperance and prudence. Their
"contract" is "too rash, too unadvised, too sudden"; it is
"like the lightning, which doth cease to be / Ere one can
say 'It lightens'" (2.2.119–20). The repetition of "lightning" and "lightens" echoes her concerns a few lines earlier that her sudden, rash, and ill-advised words might lead
Romeo to believe that she was "yielding to light love".

The connection is therefore made between the unchaste and intemperate "love" to which she is yielding and the brief but deadly storm of passion that it will unleash.

Romeo's response to Juliet's desire to bid him "good night" is as crass as ever: "O, wilt thou leave me so unsatisfied?" (2.2.125). As usual, his principle concern is with his own self-gratification. Taken aback, Juliet asks: "What satisfaction canst thou have tonight?" (2.2.126). Clearly no satisfaction is possible. The Nurse is calling from within for Juliet, and Romeo is trespassing perilously in the garden of his family's sworn enemy. Time and place are plotting against them, and circumstance is prizing them apart. The lovers, however, will not allow time, place, or circumstance to come between them. Their impatience knows no bounds and is set to destroy them. The philosopher and critic Gene Fendt accentuates the fatal and fatalistic dimension of the lovers' irrepressible impetuosity:

> Romeo and Juliet will have each other *now*, they will have the world arranged so that they can have each other *now*, or they will kill themselves *now*. The play rushes to catch up to their infinite speed; it fails, even at the terrible speed it does develop, to catch up to the demands of their passion.[8]

Similarly the Shakespearean critic Oscar James Campbell accentuates Shakespeare's acceleration of the action compared with Brooke's source poem by the changing of Brooke's months into days, thereby introducing "a sense of headlong hurry of the eager lovers".[9]

[8] Gene Fendt, *Is Hamlet a Religious Drama?* (Milwaukee: Marquette University Press, 1998), p. 25.

[9] Oscar James Campbell, ed., *The Reader's Encyclopedia of Shakespeare* (New York: MJF Books, 1966), p. 710.

The conflict between the rash and the rational is highlighted by Romeo's comparison of the desire of the lovers for each other with the disdain of a schoolboy for his books:

> Love goes toward love as school-boys from their books;
> But love from love, toward school with heavy looks.
>
> (2.2.156–57)

The lovers are equated with the reluctance of a schoolboy to learn from his elders. Like the immature schoolboy, the impetuous and equally immature lovers have no desire to grow in wisdom, knowledge, or understanding, seeking only the gratification of play. Their rashness is irrational, and their love spurns both wisdom and conscience. It is in this headlong rush from reason that the headlong rush to destruction is predicated.

The idolatrous nature of Romeo's love for Juliet is again stressed by Romeo's description of Juliet as "my soul" (2.2.165), and the ultimately unhealthy nature of their love is emphasized by the metaphor with which Shakespeare chooses to end this pivotal scene in which Juliet falls from the balcony, ultimately to her death.

> *Juliet.* 'Tis almost morning. I would have thee gone;
>   And yet no farther than a wanton's bird,
>   That lets it hop a little from his hand,
>   Like a poor prisoner in his twisted gyves,
>   And with a silk thread plucks it back again,
>   So loving-jealous of his liberty.
> *Romeo.* I would I were thy bird.
> *Juliet.*   Sweet, so would I.
>   Yet I should kill thee with much cherishing.
>
> (2.2.177–84)

The metaphor metamorphoses Juliet into a "wanton" and Romeo into her captive bird who is likened to "a poor prisoner" in chains. Although "wanton" is usually glossed as meaning a spoiled or playfully capricious child, the play on words with the better-known meaning of "wanton" as an unchaste woman is surely intentional on the playwright's part. Indeed, Juliet can clearly be seen as being wanton in both senses of the word. She is a child whose caprice is transforming her prematurely into an unchaste woman. Whereas caprice might be charming in a child, it is far less so in an adult, in which it takes on the altogether darker sexual connotations connected with its etymological connection to *capra* (goat), the beast in mediaeval typology connected to the sin of fornication.[10]

The wanton's relationship with the bird (lover) is not healthy, resulting in the latter's captivity and its prevention from living the free life to which the laws of nature imbued it. Birds are meant to fly freely, and, on a higher level, so are people, the latter of whom are meant to fly to their Creator on the wings of faith and reason (*fides et ratio*). It is through these liberating gifts that the human person is freed, via the Passion of Christ, from the bondage of sin and ignorance, thus finding the genuine freedom that is found in Christ alone. Shakespeare's employment of such a powerful metaphor at the culmination of the crucial balcony scene is indicative of

---

[10] See, for instance, Theobaldus, *Physiologus of Theobaldus*, ed. Richard Morris, in *An Old English Miscellany*, Early English Text Society 49 (London: N. Trubner, 1872). This is a translation of the mediaeval bestiary by Bishop Theobaldus. Louis Charbonneau-Lassay, in *The Bestiary of Christ*, trans. D. M. Dooling (New York: Parabola, 1991), p. 86, writes: "Although the young he-goat is a delightful and attractive animal, as it becomes sexually mature it becomes lustful and a vile odor begins to emanate from it; soon it becomes a disgusting and repugnant creature which one wishes to avoid.... Among the ancient Greeks, it was said of libidinous people that they 'smelled of goat'."

his Catholic formation, which would have been steeped in the philosophical and theological traditions of scholasticism.

As Gene Fendt reminds us, the "Renaissance and medieval are arguably closer to each other than, for example, we (post)moderns are to either of them." As such, he continues, "it is more licit to read Shakespeare next to Aquinas than next to Freud, Jung, Lacan, Foucault, et al." [11] Reading Shakespeare in the light of those whom he knew, such as Aquinas or his literary disciple Dante, is patently more honest than reading him in the light of those of whom he was blissfully unaware, such as Freud, Marx, or Derrida. In reading him in the light of his illustrious predecessors, it is difficult to escape the obvious parallels between Shakespeare's lovers and Dante's Paolo and Francesca, who are doomed to be blown around by the winds of irrational passion for eternity. Yet we should avoid simply equating the one erotically blinded couple with the other. Whereas Paolo and Francesca were adulterers, Romeo and Juliet are married before they consummate their relationship. As such, it would be premature to presume that Shakespeare's lovers deserve the eternal punishment meted out by Dante on his own unrepentant lovers. Nonetheless, the Catholic Shakespeare *is* much closer to the Catholic Dante than he is to our own deplorably "post-Christian" epoch, and he clearly implies the dangers of following eros to the detriment of caritas even if he is not necessarily inferring an infernal destiny for his self-destructive lovers.

In capturing each other's hearts, Romeo and Juliet have enslaved each other's minds and consciences. In Jane Austen's

---

[11] Fendt, *Is Hamlet a Religious Drama?*, p. 93. Fendt is referring to notions of "ecstasy" in *Hamlet*, but his conclusions are nonetheless valid in a much broader sense.

formulation of the problem, they have exchanged good sense for mere sensibility, forsaking the rational virtue of the former for the irrational fervor of the latter. This is not only foolhardy but deadly, as Juliet unwittingly intimates when she concludes her metaphorical fancy about the caging of her flightless lover: "Yet I should kill thee with much cherishing." If eros (sexual love) is not in harmony with caritas (theologically virtuous love that always seeks the good of the Other before the self) it will prove destructive to those in its grip. This is the overarching moral to which the play points.

As Juliet plummets from the balcony, she will kill the one into whose arms she flies.

6

FRIAR LAWRENCE: "WE STILL HAVE KNOWN THEE FOR A HOLY MAN"

Friar Lawrence, who makes his first appearance immediately after the pivotal balcony scene, is one of the most complex and perplexing of Shakespeare's characters. Is he, as both Juliet and the Prince believe, "a holy man" (4.3.29; 5.3.269), or is he, as some of his critics argue, a meddlesome friar who does more harm than good? Taking the former position, the German scholars Heinrich Mutschmann and Karl Wentersdorf point to the sympathetic portrayal of the Friar as evidence of the Bard's Catholicism,[1] a view that is seconded by Peter Milward:

> When the dramatist goes on to dramatize the friar, in contrast to Brooke's depiction of him as a sanctimonious pander, he goes out of his way to multiply testimonials to the honesty and sanctity of Friar Laurence. Thus, for example, Capulet respects him as a "reverend holy friar" (4.2.31); Juliet reassures herself, before taking the drug he has given her, that "he hath still been tried for a holy man" (4.3.29); and the Prince of Verona, even in the face of the friar's admission of guilt, allows for his good intentions, with an

[1] Heinrich Mutschmann and Karl Wentersdorf, *Shakespeare and Catholicism* (New York: Sheed and Ward, 1952), pp. 267–74, 281.

echo of Juliet's words, "We still have known thee for a holy man" (5.3.269).[2]

The pioneering Shakespeare scholar Henry Sebastian Bowden insists that "the Friar's advice is always in accordance with the purest morality" and adds that the Friar "agrees with Romeo's marriage with Juliet, not as an intriguing matchmaker, but as one who knows what human nature is".[3] Ian Wilson, in his excellent book *Shakespeare: The Evidence*, compares Shakespeare's sympathetic portrayal of Friar Lawrence with the way that priests and religious were portrayed in the plays of Shakespeare's contemporaries:

> Thus whereas Christopher Marlowe in his *Jew of Malta* joked about priests and monks, and in his *Massacre at Paris* spoke of "five hundred fat Franciscan friars and priests", and while Robert Greene was likewise quite undisguised in his anti-Catholic stance, Shakespeare portrays his Friar Laurence almost entirely sympathetically.[4]

Similarly we should remind ourselves of Arthur Brooke's condemnation of "superstitious friers (the naturally fitte instruments of unchastitie)" and his description of auricular confessions as "the kay of whoredome, and treason".[5]

Although Shakespeare's depiction of Friar Lawrence is indeed sympathetic, countering contemporary prejudices and indicating Shakespeare's own Catholic sympathies, it would

---

[2] Peter Milward, S.J., *Shakespeare the Papist* (Ave Maria, Fla.: Sapientia Press, 2005), p. 73.

[3] Quoted in Ian Wilson, *Shakespeare: The Evidence* (New York: St. Martin's Griffin, 1999), p. 197.

[4] Wilson, *Shakespeare: The Evidence*, pp. 196–97.

[5] Arthur Brooke, *The Tragicall Historye of Romeus and Juliet* (1562), in Geoffrey Bullough, ed., *Narrative and Dramatic Sources of Shakespeare*, vol. 1 (London: Routledge, 1957). In fairness, Brooke's poem is not as harsh on the Friar as his polemical preface might suggest.

be wrong to suggest that the Friar's role is unproblematic. Take, for instance, his opening speech when he is introduced to us as both a philosopher and an herbalist:

> O, mickle is the powerful grace that lies
> In plants, herbs, stones, and their true qualities;
> For nought so vile that on the earth doth live
> But to the earth some special good doth give;
> Nor aught so good but, strain'd from that fair use,
> Revolts from true birth, stumbling on abuse:
> Virtue itself turns vice, being misapplied,
> And vice sometime's by action dignified.
>   *Enter Romeo.*
> Within the infant rind of this weak flower
> Poison hath residence, and medicine power;
> For this, being smelt, with that part cheers each part;
> Being tasted, stays all senses with the heart.
> Two such opposed kings encamp them still
> In man as well as herbs—grace and rude will;
> And where the worser is predominant,
> Full soon the canker death eats up that plant.
>   (2.3.15–30)

Jonathan Marks reads this passage as a betrayal of a fatal flaw in the Friar's philosophy, one which motivates his manipulation of the passions of the young lovers:

> Friar Lawrence reads virtue and vice, grace and rebellion, into nature. But he thinks that the virtue or vice of things depends on their right or wrong use and that he is capable of distinguishing between right and wrong use, and even of transforming vice into virtue, through his knowledge. Virtue and vice, grace and rebellion, are objects to be manipulated by the knower of nature.

The Friar's activities suggest that he thinks he can use human beings just as he uses herbs. He attempts to use Romeo and Juliet to make peace between the Montagues and Capulets, concerning himself more with this objective than with the souls of the young lovers.[6]

Other critics take this view of the manipulative Friar even further, interpreting his opening speech as a "hymn to power".[7] Peter Milward, taking a contrary view, sees the opening speech as containing "a deep Christian wisdom that is aptly related both to his religious profession, as a 'holy Franciscan friar' (5.2.1), and to the dramatic function he is to fulfill".[8] Comparing the Friar with the exiled duke in *As You Like It* who sees "good in everything" (2.1.17), Milward suggests that the Friar's words echo those of Thomas à Kempis in *The Imitation of Christ*, a book that was hugely popular in Elizabethan England, being twice translated and being published in numerous editions. In particular, Milward argues that the Friar's observation that "nought so vile that on the earth doth live, / but to the earth some special good doth give" is a rephrasing of the words of à Kempis that "there is no creature so small and vile, but shows forth the goodness of God."[9] Furthermore, Milward contends that the Friar's reference to the "opposed kings" that "encamp them still / In man as well as herbs—grace and rude will" is a recollection

[6] Jonathan Marks, "Fools for Love? Shakespeare's Qualified Defense of *Romeo and Juliet*", in William Shakespeare, *Romeo and Juliet*, ed. Joseph Pearce, Ignatius Critical Editions (San Francisco: Ignatius Press, 2011), p. 224.

[7] See Gerry Brenner, "Shakespeare's Politically Ambitious Friar", *Shakespeare Studies* 13 (1980): 51; and Jerry Weinberger, "Pious Princes and Red Hot Lovers: The Politics of Shakespeare's *Romeo and Juliet*", *The Journal of Politics* 65 (May 2003): 350–75.

[8] Milward, *Shakespeare the Papist*, p. 74.

[9] Thomas à Kempis, *The Imitation of Christ* (Redford, Va.: Wilder, 2008), p. 35.

of the meditation in the *Spiritual Exercises* of Saint Ignatius Loyola on "The Two Standards" of Christ and Satan.[10]

Although, and as we shall see, there are problems attached to many of the decisions that Friar Lawrence makes, to see his opening speech as a "hymn to power" is untenable, except in the sense that it is a hymn to the power of God made manifest in his creatures. For all its references to *The Imitation of Christ* and its possible allusions to the *Spiritual Exercises*, the charism that animates the Friar's speech is ultimately that of the religious order to which he belongs. One sees in his words a clear reflection of Saint Francis' "Canticle of the Sun":

> Be praised, my Lord, through all your creatures, especially through my lord Brother Sun, who brings the day; and you give light through him. And he is beautiful and radiant in all his splendor! Of you, Most High, he bears the likeness.
>
> Be praised, my Lord, through Sister Moon and the stars; in the heavens you have made them, precious and beautiful.
>
> Be praised, my Lord, through Brothers Wind and Air, and clouds and storms, and all the weather, through which you give your creatures sustenance.
>
> Be praised, My Lord, through Sister Water; she is very useful, and humble, and precious, and pure.
>
> Be praised, my Lord, through Brother Fire, through whom you brighten the night. He is beautiful and cheerful, and powerful and strong.
>
> Be praised, my Lord, through our sister Mother Earth, who feeds us and rules us, and produces various fruits with colored flowers and herbs.

[10] Ibid.

As with Saint Francis' Canticle, Friar Lawrence's speech begins with praise for "Brother Sun, who brings the day" and through whom God gives his light:

> The gray-ey'd morn smiles on the frowning night,
> Check'ring the eastern clouds with streaks of light;
> And fleckel'd darkness like a drunkard reels
> From forth day's path and Titan's fiery wheels.
> Now, ere the sun advance his burning eye
> The day to cheer and night's dank dew to dry,
> I must up-fill this osier cage of ours
> With baleful weeds and precious-juiced flowers.
>
> (2.3.1–8)

His very next line refers to the earth as "nature's mother", echoing Saint Francis' lines that "Mother Earth" is "our sister ... who feeds us and rules us, and produces various fruits with colored flowers and herbs". It is, therefore, appropriate that Shakespeare's Franciscan should then wax lyrical about "the powerful grace that lies / In plants, herbs, stones, and their true qualities". He is speaking not as a power-hungry manipulator of men but as a nature-loving follower of Saint Francis. Far from being ambitious in the worldly sense, he is so poor that even the basket that he carries is not his but *ours* ("this osier cage of ours"), belonging to the Franciscan order, to which he has pledged himself in poverty, chastity, and obedience. Shakespeare's own reverence for Franciscan spirituality is evident most notably in *King Lear*, where it is seen in the spirituality of Poor Tom, who sings a Franciscan ballad to signify his symbolic connection to Saint Francis, and in the climactic moment of Lear's conversion to holy poverty on the heath, which parallels the conversion of Saint Francis from worldliness to mendicancy.[11]

Friar Lawrence's reference to the "opposed kings" (2.3.27) that are encamped in man as well as herbs, "grace and rude will" (2.3.28), is not suggestive of a heretical dualism on the Friar's part, as some critics have suggested, but is merely indicative of his orthodox belief that everything in nature, men and herbs alike, are full of God's grace and yet fallen; everything is kept in existence by God's love for his creation, and yet everything is subject to entropy and death. Everything shares in its Maker's beauty and goodness, yet everything is marred by the Fall. This, the very crux of life's mystery, is understood by the Friar and is expressed by him with true eloquence and thoroughgoing orthodoxy.

All of the foregoing serves as the spiritual backdrop to the scene, introducing us to the sanctity of the Friar, but its real dramatic purpose is not evident until we see the Friar's words in relation to Romeo, who enters, significantly, in the very middle of the Friar's philosophical monologue.

The Friar's words immediately before the arrival of Romeo remind us that there is nothing "so good but, strain'd from that fair use, / Revolts from true birth, stumbling on abuse" (2.3.19–20). On the human level, we are all good, insofar as we are made by God in his image, whereas our sins are a revolution against our true birthright. Rejecting virtue, the "fair use" of our lives, we fall through our sinful choices, "stumbling on abuse". Thus, the Friar continues:

---

[11] For a full discussion of the Franciscan elements in *King Lear*, see Joseph Pearce, *Through Shakespeare's Eyes: Seeing the Catholic Presence in the Plays* (San Francisco: Ignatius Press, 2010).

> Virtue itself turns vice, being misapplied,
> And vice sometime's by action dignified.
>
> (2.3.21–22)

Once again, the Friar's words are profoundly orthodox, echoing the teaching of Saint Augustine and Saint Thomas Aquinas on the relationship between vice and virtue. Since evil only exists as a privation, as a loss or absence of the good, vice only exists in relation to the virtue of which it is the loss. Furthermore, and more specific to the case of the imminently arriving Romeo, sins of incontinence are the result of an uncontrolled or "misapplied" appetite. Thus, in Romeo's case, the virtue of love turns to vice when he fails to apply the necessary virtues of chastity, prudence, and temperance. The Friar's words, and their relationship to Romeo's actions, are best explained through an analogy with Paolo and Francesca in Dante's *Inferno*. In her notes to the *Inferno*, Dorothy L. Sayers discusses the significance of the Circles of Incontinence in Dante's hell, the first of which is the circle of the lustful:

> This and the next three circles are devoted to those who sinned less by deliberate choice of evil than by failure to make resolute choice of the good. Here are the sins of self-indulgence, weakness of will, and easy yielding to appetite ... Lust is a type of *shared* sin; at its best, and so long as it remains a sin of incontinence only, there is mutuality in it and exchange: although, in fact, mutual indulgence only serves to push both parties along the road to Hell, it is not, in intention, wholly selfish. For this reason Dante, with perfect orthodoxy, rates it as the least hateful of the deadly sins. (Sexual sins in which love and mutuality have no part find their place far below.)[12]

---

[12] Dante, *The Divine Comedy, Part 1: Hell*, trans. Dorothy L. Sayers (London: Penguin Classics, 1949), p. 101.

Sayers' depiction of the sins of the lustful in general, and Paolo and Francesca in particular, are a fair reflection of the sins of Romeo and Juliet. Their sins are those of "self-indulgence, weakness of will, and easy yielding to appetite". Theirs is very much a "*shared* sin". It has "mutuality in it and exchange" and "is not, in intention, wholly selfish". Note also that Dante distinguishes between the lustful love of Paolo and Francesca, whose shared vice is "the least hateful of the deadly sins", and the loveless sexual acts of others whom Dante places much lower in hell. The irony is that the modern world also distinguishes between these two types of sexual relationship and has decided that the first is no longer a sin because the partners in crime are deemed to be "in love". This is not Dante's position, nor is it Shakespeare's, both of whom, as Catholics, saw unchaste love as defective and deficient, and ultimately deadly. This is not to say that they could not sympathize with the sinners. Shakespeare's tender and delicate treatment of his two lovers has led many modern readers to conclude that he condones their actions, just as many modern readers have sought to liberate Paolo and Francesca from hell. Yet, as Sayers explains, Dante's sympathy for the plight of his lovers does not constitute an exoneration or a condoning of their sins:

> Tender and beautiful as Dante's handling of Francesca is, he has sketched her with a deadly accuracy. All the good is there; the charm, the courtesy, the instant response to affection, the grateful eagerness to please; but also all the evil; the easy yielding, the inability to say No, the intense self-pity.[13]

Similarly, Charles Williams, in *The Figure of Beatrice*, insists that we must not allow the poet's tenderness in his treatment of Paolo and Francesca to eclipse his moral purpose:

[13] Ibid., p. 102.

[T]he episode of Paolo and Francesca ... is always quoted
as an example of Dante's tenderness. So, no doubt, it is,
but it is not here for that reason.... It has a much more
important place; it presents the first tender, passionate, and
half-excusable consent of the soul to sin.... Dante himself
sighs to think "how many sweet thoughts, how great a desire,
brought them to this dolorous state". What indeed was the
sin? It was a forbidden love? yes, but Dante ... does not
leave it at that. He so manages the description, he so height-
ens the excuse, that the excuse reveals itself as precisely the
sin. The old name for lechery is *luxuria; lussuria* is the word
Virgil uses of this circle, and it is *lussuria*, luxury, indulgence, self-yielding, which is the sin, and the opening out
of hell. The persistent parleying with the occasion of sin,
the sweet prolonged laziness of love, is the first surrender of
the soul to hell—small but certain. The formal sin here is
the adultery of the two lovers; the poetic sin is their shrinking from the adult love demanded of them.[14]

The parallels between Dante's lovers and Shakespeare's
are palpable, but let's make the necessary distinctions. The
love between Paolo and Francesca was "forbidden" because
Francesca was married. As such, their act was one of adultery. The love between Romeo and Juliet is "forbidden"
because of the enmity that exists between their two families. There is, therefore, no adultery involved. Yet, as Williams reminds us, Dante does not condemn his lovers to
hell simply for their adultery. It is the luxury, indulgence,
and self-yielding, which is the sin. They are in the circle of
the lustful not the circle of adulterers. The other distinction we might want to make in Juliet's defense, if not necessarily in Romeo's, is that she is hardly mature enough to

[14] Charles Williams, *The Figure of Beatrice* (Berkeley, Calif.: Apocryphile
Press, 2005), pp. 117–18.

be blamed for "shrinking from the adult love demanded of them". Nonetheless, and to reiterate, the parallels are palpable, not least because Shakespeare is far closer to Dante in terms of their shared theology and philosophy than he is to those who view the lovers through the romantically tinted rose-colored spectacles of our own luxuriating and self-indulgent epoch. It is, therefore, in this light that we must understand Friar Lawrence's lament that "virtue itself turns vice, being misapplied" (2.3.21). More problematic perhaps is the line with which the Friar couples this one: "And vice sometime's by action dignified" (2.3.22). Although this line is sometimes taken to have a dualistic meaning, suggesting that evil can be dignified, it is clear within the wider context of the orthodoxy of the rest of the soliloquy that he is saying that good can be brought from evil through the power or "action" of grace, and through the good actions of those cooperating with grace. Within the context of the imminent arrival of Romeo, the Friar's words might also be seen as a portentous reference to his own ultimately disastrous role in the saga about to unfold.

It is at this very moment that Romeo enters the stage, seen by us but not by the Friar.

Having cued Romeo with the couplet about virtue turning to vice and the necessity of good actions to mollify the effects of evil, the remainder of Friar Lawrence's monologue is pregnant with moral references to Romeo's state of soul in the wake of his recent actions. The fact that the audience can see Romeo, whereas the Friar is as yet unaware of his presence, is symbolic of the fact that the Friar is unconscious of the allegorical significance of his words, whereas we are privy to them. It is as though the playwright asks his audience to behold the man to whom the Friar's words are unwittingly pointing:

Within the infant rind of this weak flower
Poison hath residence, and medicine power;
For this, being smelt, with that part cheers each part;
Being tasted, slays all senses with the heart.
Two such opposed kings encamp them still
In man as well as herbs—grace and rude will;
And where the worser is predominant,
Full soon the canker death eats up that plant.

(2.3.23–30)

Since Romeo has just walked on stage, the Friar's reference to "this weak flower" is clearly applicable to the feckless and febrile lover, whose "infant rind" (soul) contains a resident "poison" (sinfulness) as well as powerful "medicine" (virtue). The fragrance of virtue has healing qualities, whereas the taste of sin is deadly. And lest his audience should miss the point, Shakespeare then has his friar spell out the analogy and allegory for us. These qualities are to be found "in man as well as herbs". Virtue is the rightful response of the soul to "grace"; vice is the rebellious refusal of grace through the pursuit of "rude will". His point being made in no uncertain terms, the Friar's final moral flourish is a veritable *coup de grâce*:

And where the worser is predominant,
Full soon the canker death eats up that plant.

(2.3.29–30)

Where "rude will" predominates over "grace" a cancerous death "full soon" awaits the sinner.

Having greeted Romeo as "this weak flower", the Friar ends with a prophetic premonition of the death awaiting "that plant". As Romeo appears, the Friar's metaphorical soliloquy has left us in no doubt that the rude and willful lover is leading himself and his betrothed into mortal danger.

7

"MYSELF CONDEMNED AND MYSELF EXCUS'D": THE VICE AND VIRTUE OF FRIAR LAWRENCE

Following Friar Lawrence's allegorical references to the newly arrived Romeo, the Friar learns that Romeo is newly in love with "the fair daughter of rich Capulet" (2.3.58). Furthermore, with the rashness and intemperance that has defined Romeo's character from the outset, the young lover beseeches the Friar "to marry us to-day" (2.3.64). The Friar's response is full of the fruit of Christian wisdom:

> Holy Saint Francis! What a change is here!
> Is Rosaline, that thou didst love so dear,
> So soon forsaken? Young men's love, then, lies
> Not truly in their hearts, but in their eyes.
> Jesu Maria, what a deal of brine
> Hath wash'd thy sallow cheeks for Rosaline!
> How much salt water thrown away in waste,
> To season love, that of it doth not taste!
> The sun not yet thy sighs from heaven clears,
> Thy old groans yet ringing in my ancient ears;
> Lo, here upon thy cheek the stain doth sit
> Of an old tear that is not wash'd off yet.
> If e'er thou wast thyself, and these woes thine,

Thou and these woes were all for Rosaline.
And art thou chang'd? Pronounce this sentence, then:
Women may fall, when there's no strength in men.

(2.3.65–80)

Invoking Jesus, Mary, and Saint Francis, the Friar exclaims
in exasperation that Romeo's declarations of love for Juliet
seem dubious and even indecent so soon after his similar
declarations for the "so soon forsaken" Rosaline: "Young
men's love, then, lies / Not truly in their hearts, but in their
eyes." The superficiality of Romeo's love is emphasized by
the wordplay on "lies". His love lies. It is not true. The
sallowness of Romeo's cheeks, washed white with tears that
are forgotten as swiftly as his former love is forsaken, is a
reflection of the shallowness of his love. The fact that such
love, though tasting sweet, can be a deadly poison, or mortal sin, is driven home by the portentous (death) sentence
that the Friar pronounces at the conclusion of his speech:
"Pronounce this sentence then: / Women may fall, when
there's no strength in men." Romeo's weakness and the weak
love that is its consequence will lead to the fall of the woman
that he claims to love. In Romeo's weakness is Juliet's fall,
though Juliet's own weakness contributes to their shared
culpability.

Romeo acknowledges that the Friar had chided him "oft
for loving Rosaline", to which the Friar responds that he
was chiding Romeo for "doting, not for loving" (2.3.81–
82). It was the falseness or shallowness of his love that was
being chided, not love itself. Ever oblivious of sage advice,
Romeo responds blithely that the Friar had "bad'st me bury
love" (2.3.83), to which the Friar responds that he didn't
intend Romeo to bury one love in order to unearth another
in its place (2.3.83–85). Clearly the Friar is equating Romeo's

love for Rosaline with his new love for Juliet, a misunderstanding, as Romeo sees it, that the besotted lover is at pains to correct:

> I pray thee chide me not; her I love now
> Doth grace for grace and love for love allow;
> The other did not so.

> (2.3.85–87)

Once again, Romeo condemns himself with his own words. He does not refute the Friar's concerns by insisting that the nature of his love for Juliet is different from that which he had for Rosaline, conceding that his love for Rosaline was indeed false but that his love for Juliet is true. On the contrary, his words suggest that the only difference between the two loves is that Juliet was receptive to his romantic advances, allowing "love for love", whereas Rosaline had rebuffed him. Romeo's love, or the lack thereof, is the same in both cases; the difference is in the reaction of the two women to it. Rosaline is unmoved by Romeo's Petrarchan platitudes and is therefore untouched by the ensuing tragedy; Juliet succumbs to the poetic charm and is tangled in the tragic web.

Up to this point in the drama, Friar Lawrence has acquitted himself with commendable rectitude and gracious aplomb. Now, however, he seems to succumb to the same rashness and impetuosity that recurs as a curse throughout the entirety of the play. Having chided the young lover for the fallacious and fatuous nature of his love, he agrees to marry Romeo and Juliet on the grounds that "this alliance may ... turn your households' rancour to pure love" (2.3.91–92). Apart from the Friar's perilous naïveté in imagining that a clandestine marriage, conducted without the parents' knowledge or consent, would foster harmony, we are shocked to see the Friar acting as rashly, and therefore as irrationally, in his blind pursuit of "peace" as are the young couple in their blind pursuit of "love". In his defense, we should recall Henry Sebastian Bowden's claim that "the Friar's advice is always in accordance with the purest morality" and that the Friar "agrees with Romeo's marriage with Juliet, not as an intriguing matchmaker, but as one who knows what human nature is" (see p. 65 above). One can only assume that Bowden, a Catholic priest, had the First Epistle of Saint Paul to the Corinthians in mind, in which the apostle states that those who cannot contain their passions should marry because "it is better to marry than to burn" (1 Cor 7:9).[1] If the Friar believes that Romeo is incapable of tempering his passionate desires, which seems likely considering Romeo's complete lack of self-control, he might consider that marriage is the only way of keeping his young charge from mortal sin. This understanding of the Friar's motives would seem to be supported by the last words he says before he marries the impassioned couple:

Come, come with me, and we will make short work;
For, by your leaves, you shall not stay alone
Till holy church incorporate two in one.

(2.6.35–37)

Clearly the Friar believes that the lovers are not safe to be left alone together and that the bonds of marriage can save them from themselves and from the mortal sin of fornication. This pastoral consideration, reinforced by the hope

[1] This is the KJV translation. The Douai Rheims translation reads: "But if they do not contain themselves, let them marry. For it is better to marry than to be burnt." Other translations, spurning understatement in pursuit of graphic expostulation, incorporate the phrase "burn with lust" or "burn with sexual desire".

that the marriage might bring peace between the feuding families, could explain the Friar's motive for agreeing to the nuptial union. It is, however, not a sufficient or convincing excuse for his complicity in the ill-advised and ultimately destructive marriage.

The irony inherent in the disconnectedness between the wisdom of the Friar's philosophy and the foolishness of his actions is conveyed in the final lines of the scene. Having agreed to marry Romeo and Juliet, in contradiction of all the sagacious words that he spoke prior to the rash announcement, Friar Lawrence is faced with Romeo's impatience: "O, let us hence; I stand on sudden haste." "Wisely and slow", the Friar replies. "They stumble that run fast" (2.3.93– 95). The "sudden haste" of Romeo does not surprise us. He has not stopped for breath (or to think) since the play began. What does surprise us is the Friar's counsel to proceed slowly and with wisdom. Only seconds earlier he had acquiesced in Romeo's desire to be married in secret that very day to a young girl, not yet fourteen years of age, whom Romeo had met the night before. Where is the wisdom in such folly? Where is the slowness required for patient and prudent deliberation? Clearly the Friar's final words are charged with unwitting irony. His failure to practice what he preached will cause the action of the drama to accelerate out of control. Lacking the wisdom and slowness that it is the Friar's duty to bestow, the young lovers will run so fast that they will not only stumble but fall headlong to their own destruction.

The dissonance between the Friar's wisdom and his foolish actions demands further attention and has been the subject of much critical discussion and debate. Stephen Zelnick highlights how the Friar's actions were not in conformity with the teaching of the Church:

In 1563, at the Council of Trent, the Catholic Church adopted the public announcement of the banns of marriage as standard Church practice. The council was concerned about clandestine marriages, that is, marriages performed without public notice and without the knowledge of the couple's families. While this requirement would not have been in force in renaissance Verona, the problem and dangers were well understood in Shakespeare's time. With Romeo and Juliet's desperate desire to be married, the Friar faces what should be a difficult choice. While the feud explains their need for secrecy, it should explain also the Friar's need to exercise caution. Instead, the Friar serves the immediate desire of the lovers while imagining that in doing so he will somehow reconcile the families and bring peace to Verona.[2]

Zelnick's provision of the historical context accentuates still further the irresponsible folly of the Friar's decision to marry the young couple, especially when the shocking reality of Juliet's extreme youth is also taken into account. As Zelnick emphasizes, these factors should have caused the Friar to "exercise caution" or, to employ the Friar's own words, to proceed "wisely and slow". Instead he proceeds with the "sudden haste" that Romeo urges and, in so doing, inadvertently facilitates the disastrous consequences that the Friar's own Christian philosophy prophesies.

At this juncture we might wish to urge in the Friar's defense that he was well-meaning and that his desire to bring peace between the feuding families is laudable. Indeed, to employ analogies from the popular culture of our own time, the Friar acts as he does because he wants to "give peace a

[2] Stephen Zelnick, "*Romeo and Juliet*: The 'True Ground of All These Piteous Woes'", in William Shakespeare, *Romeo and Juliet*, ed. Joseph Pearce, Ignatius Critical Editions (San Francisco: Ignatius Press, 2011), p. 250.

chance" in much the same way as the relationship between Romeo and Juliet is permissible because "all you need is love". Yet, as we have seen, Shakespeare dives deeper than the shallow interpretations of romanticism, and offers thereby a timeless warning against the illusory and vacuous "peace and love" of Lennon and his ilk.[3] Rooted in the profundity of Christian philosophy, Shakespeare was aware that it was always illicit to use immoral means to an ostensibly moral end. As the critic Jill Kriegel explains, "[the Friar's] plan to heal the evil of the feud using deception is unsound, and his words are at variance with his actions."[4]

With regard to the consequences of the Friar's folly to the subsequent tragic denouement of the plot, it can best be summarized in a famous poetic aphorism sometimes attributed to Shakespeare but actually originating with Sir Walter Scott: "Oh what a tangled web we weave / When first we practice to deceive."[5] Stephen Zelnick, discussing the Friar's role in the tragedy, puts the matter more prosaically: "Once deceptions start, where do they end?"[6]

> As the Friar's involvement deepens, his counsels become more dangerous. When Juliet, at the news of Romeo's banishment, tells the Friar she will kill herself, the good Friar takes this cue and devises his plan to administer a drug with effects that mimic death. This desperate plan requires that

[3] The Beatles' "All You Need Is Love" is John Lennon's anthem to "free love", i.e., love without responsibility, whereas "Give Peace a Chance", Lennon's pacifist mantra, is a demand for "free peace", i.e., peace without responsibility. Lennon, like the Byronic romantics who preceded him, is making a virtue of self-indulgence.

[4] Jill Kriegel, "A Case against Natural Magic: Shakespeare's Friar Lawrence as *Romeo and Juliet*'s Near-Tragic Hero", in Shakespeare, *Romeo and Juliet*, ed. Pearce, p. 212.

[5] Sir Walter Scott, *Marmion* (1808), canto 6, stanza 17.

[6] Zelnick, "*Romeo and Juliet*: The 'True Ground'", p. 251.

several uncontrollable pieces fall into place. The Friar's plot involves also a conspiracy of lies and deceptions—this from the man who counsels moderation, caution, and the consolations of philosophy. Nor is the deception merely passive: the Friar lies to the Capulets, even as they suffer through the apparent death of their daughter (4.5.64–76). Yet the worst charge against Friar Lawrence is his cowardice. Once Romeo is banished, the Friar should step forward to announce Romeo's marriage to Juliet to the respective families and personally face their displeasure. Worse yet, when Juliet awakens in the tomb—Romeo already dead by poison, and she about to discover this devastating fact the Friar runs off, fearful he will be discovered as a part of the plot.[7]

The shocking discrepancy between the faith-filled wisdom of the Friar's words and the deceitful and cowardly nature of his actions is the catalyst that makes the cataclysmic climax possible. "Friar Lawrence knows the fault is not in the stars but in himself, that everything miscarried by his fault, and that in his readiness to do good, by reconciling the feuding families, he had allowed his goodwill to overwhelm his duty to his community." [8]

Jill Kriegel argues that Friar Lawrence, "through his negative example", provides a vital moral lesson:

It is true, as [Peter] Milward maintains, that through Friar Laurence, Shakespeare instills the play with "a deep Christian wisdom that is aptly related ... to [the Friar's] religious profession",[9] but through him we also see the weakness of every man—weakness that is healed only by admission,

[7] Ibid., p. 250.
[8] Ibid., p. 251.
[9] Peter Milward, S.J., *Christian Themes in English Literature* (Tokyo: Kenkyusha, 1967), p. 55.

confession, and atonement. Friar Lawrence relinquishes control, admitting "[a] greater power than we can contradict / Hath thwarted our intents" (5.3.153–54), confessing all that was "[m]iscarried by [his] fault" (266), and atoning with an offering of his life for his sins. Thus we can agree with the Prince's absolving decree: "We have still known thee for a holy man" (269) and know that Friar Laurence's newly regained humility, faith, and reason—if realized earlier— could have saved Juliet, and thus her Romeo.[10]

In sharing Kriegel's perception of the positive moral lesson to be learned from the Friar's negative example, and mindful of the parallels between Romeo and Juliet and Paolo and Francesca, we are reminded of Chaucer's Prologue to *The Canterbury Tales* in which the negative examples of the bad and wayward characters merely serve to highlight the sanctity of the Parson and the Ploughman:

> For if a priest be foul, on whom we trust,
> No wonder is a lewed man to rust:
> And shame it is, if that a priest take keep,
> To see a shitten shepherd and clean sheep:
> Well ought a priest ensample for to give,
> By his own cleanness, how his sheep should live.[11]

Ultimately, however, the Friar is not to be likened to the "shitten shepherd", and still less to the sundry religious reprobates that Chaucer places amongst his Canterbury pilgrims. On the contrary, the Friar is never cynical or self-seeking even in his foolishness and moreover and most importantly is a genuinely chastened penitent in the play's

---

[10] Kriegel, "Case against Natural Magic", p. 215.
[11] Geoffrey Chaucer, prologue to *The Canterbury Tales* (New York: W. W. Norton, 1989), p. 15.

final scene, a fact that is made manifest in the final lines he utters:

> And if aught in this
> Miscarried by my fault, let my old life
> Be sacrific'd, some hour before his time,
> Unto the rigour of severest law.
>
> (5.3.265–68)

Moving from a mediaeval to a modern parallel, Friar Law rence can be likened more justly to the character of Boromir in *The Lord of the Rings*, who betrays the Fellowship in order to save his own people (as he sees it), thereby succumbing to evil means to a good end, much as the Friar acts imprudently and rashly in the cause of restoring "peace" to the streets of Verona. Boromir repents of his sin and accepts death as his just punishment, much as the Friar embraces the death sentence, "the rigour of severest law", if the Prince should decide that he should be punished for his role in the tragic turn of events. Boromir's repentance is seen by his comrades as washing away any traces of culpability, much as the Prince insists that "[w]e still have known thee for a holy man" (5 3 269) at the end of the Friar's final speech.

With the Prince's words fresh in our minds we should conclude our discussion of Friar Lawrence by revisiting the question that was posed at the beginning of the last chapter: Is Friar Lawrence, as both Juliet and the Prince believe, "a holy man", or is he, as some of his critics argue, a meddlesome friar who does more harm than good? Having put the case for the "holy man" in the previous chapter, and the case for the "meddlesome friar" in this chapter, we can perhaps conclude by stating that he is both. He is an agent of grace in the wisdom of his words and an agent of disgrace in the folly of his actions. If he had better practiced the Franciscan virtue and Christian philosophy that he preached, his role would have been entirely beneficial and benevolent, and, no doubt, the tragedy could have been avoided. Yet even in his abject failure, he remains paradoxically, unwittingly, providentially, and even miraculously the "instrument of peace". Reflecting the famous "prayer for peace" of Saint Francis, in which the saint prays to be made an "instrument of peace", sowing love where there is hatred, the Friar's actions inadvertently bring about the peace between the feuding families that he had desired, though not of course in the manner he had envisaged.

Like Hamlet and Lear in the denouements of Shakespeare's later works, the Friar comes to realize that the hidden hand of providence has overseen the action: "A greater power than we can contradict / Hath thwarted our intents" (5.3.153–54). This ineffable presence thwarts the intentions of Romeo and Juliet's intemperate and tempestuous passion, and nullifies the schemes of the naïvely peace-seeking Friar. And yet, ironically, the Friar's folly and the lovers' fall bring the peace that the Friar had sought. Out of the darkness of the tragedy, the majestic movement of the divine hand, invisible and inviolable, restores peace to Verona. The Capulets and the Montagues are reconciled in the shadow of the suicidal despair of their children. Light emerges from the very abyss of the tomb. The "greater power" of God brings ineffable good from inestimable evil.

8

"VIOLENT DELIGHTS HAVE VIOLENT ENDS"

> *Friar Lawrence.* So smile the heavens upon this holy act
> That after-hours with sorrow chide us not!
> *Romeo.* Amen, amen! But come what sorrow can,
> It cannot countervail the exchange of joy
> That one short minute gives me in her sight.
> Do thou but close our hands with holy words,
> Then love-devouring death do what he dare;
> It is enough I may but call her mine.
> *Friar Lawrence.* These violent delights have violent ends,
> And in their triumph die; like fire and powder,
> Which, as they kiss, consume. The sweetest honey
> Is loathsome in his own deliciousness,
> And in the taste confounds the appetite.
> Therefore love moderately: long love doth so.
> Too swift arrives as tardy as too slow.
>
> (2.6.1–15)

This exchange between Romeo and Friar Lawrence, moments before the arrival of Juliet for the clandestine wedding ceremony, is pregnant with the palpitating presence of the moral dynamic animating the whole drama. The Friar prays that their actions will be blessed and that they will not be chided in the future for the folly of their actions. Romeo assents to the prayer with his "amen" but contradicts it instantly with the qualifying "but":

> Amen, amen! But come what sorrow can,
> It cannot countervail the exchange of joy
> That one short minute gives me in her sight.

Although we might perceive his words as an echo of the wedding vow, declaring that he will love his wife in good times or bad, his very next words almost defy providence to do its worst. Let him be but married to Juliet for "one short minute" and "love-devouring death" can "do what he dare". There is also the implicit suggestion that his love is false, in spite of its passionate zeal, or at least that it is not love in the fullest Christian sense. Indeed, it could be argued that his "love" is the very inverse of Christian love. The death-devouring love of the Christian is the antithesis of the "love-devouring death" of Romeo. His love does not transcend death—it is killed by it. According to his own passionate and death-defying declaration, his love for Juliet will not last forever but only for the few short days until it is extinguished by their suicide. It is scarcely surprising, therefore, that the Friar should warn him that "[t]hese violent delights have violent ends" and more than fitting that the Friar should liken the kiss of the two lovers to the explosively destructive kiss of fire and gunpowder. And yet we know that Romeo will not heed the Friar's advice to "love moderately" because "[l]ong love doth so." We perceive that Romeo's intemperate and tempestuous nature is incapable of "long love", and we simply cannot imagine that he is capable of submitting himself to the responsibilities and sacrifices of marriage, let alone to the demands of parenthood. One is even tempted to discern that Romeo would be likely to cast Juliet aside as lightly as he had discarded the all-too-soon forgotten Rosaline. One might even dare to suggest, without undue cynicism, that the only way that

Romeo could be true to his bride "till death do us part" was if death came quickly.

As for Juliet, her arrival is heralded by the Friar with words that damn with faint praise:

> Here comes the lady. O, so light a foot
> Will ne'er wear out the everlasting flint.
> A lover may bestride the gossamer
> That idles in the wanton summer air
> And yet not fall, so light is vanity.
>
> (2.6.16–20)

Physically, the arriving lady, "so light a foot", graces us with her presence, gliding across the stage with balletic sang-froid. Metaphysically, however, it is not the lightness of her movement but the lightness of her morals that grabs our attention. She doesn't touch the ground because she is gliding on the wings of pride, or vanity. Indeed, "so light is vanity" that it will never be grounded in "the everlasting flint" of bedrock reality; it will never "wear out" or wear itself out on the eternal verities that govern the life of man. It is lighter than air because it lacks substance; it floats because it lacks the gravity necessary to touch the ground. It is, therefore, not the lightness of her foot but the lightness of her vanity that arrests our attention as Juliet arrives for her fateful and fatal marriage.

Such is the breathless recklessness of the lovers that Shakespeare barely allows us to catch our breath before the joy of the clandestine wedding ceremony is shattered. In the very next scene, the cynically mercurial Mercutio is slain by the irrepressibly irascible Tybalt. Seeking revenge and blaming Juliet's beauty for making him "effeminate" (3.1.111), Romeo slays Tybalt in a fit of unbridled fury, his hatred proving more real than his love. In hatred, as in love, Romeo's impetuosity proves destructive, not merely to his adversary but to his bride. Indeed, his act of violence is also an act of infidelity. Betraying Juliet not with a kiss but with a curse upon her kinsman, he plunges the sword into the heart of their marriage as surely as he plunges it into the heart of Tybalt. Realizing this, he cries out in inconsolable anguish: "O, I am fortune's fool!" (3.1.133). He is indeed a fool, not merely in his actions but in his unconscionable shifting of the blame for his actions onto fate or "fortune" rather than on his own unwillingness to temper his passions. He and not "fortune" is to blame for his foolishness. In hatred, as in love, "violent delights have violent ends", the indulging of the passions reaping destructive consequences.

9

"IF LOVE BE BLIND,
IT BEST AGREES WITH NIGHT"

Spread thy close curtain, love-performing night,
That runaways' eyes may wink, and Romeo
Leap to these arms, untalk'd of and unseen.
Lovers can see to do their amorous rites
By their own beauties; or if love be blind,
It best agrees with night. Come, civil night,
Thou sober-suited matron, all in black ...
Come, night; come, Romeo; come, thou day in night;
For thou wilt lie upon the wings of night
Whiter than new snow on a raven's back.
Come, gentle night, come, loving, black-brow'd night,
Give me my Romeo; and, when he shall die,
Take him and cut him out in little stars,
And he will make the face of heaven so fine
That all the world will be in love with night,
And pay no worship to the garish sun.

(3.2.5–25)

As Juliet awaits her Romeo with mounting excitement and
expectation, she is unaware that his slaying of her cousin
has cast a doom-cloud over their marriage. She is in the
dark and, impatient for the coming of night, is blissfully

unaware that the night has already descended. The news of Tybalt's death, imminently to be delivered by the Nurse, will plunge the lover of night into utter darkness. Since we, as readers or as audience, are privy to the tragedy of which Juliet is as yet unaware, her words are charged with irony. Yet there is more to the nocturnal imagery than the portentous descent of tragic darkness. Apart from the literal necessity of darkness to conceal their secret love from their respective families, the imagery relates to the very essence of their love, which shuns the light in its utter self-absorption: "Lovers can see to do their amorous rites / By their own beauties". Only having eyes for each other, the lovers have no need of any light beyond their own self-absorbed world. They *are* the light by which they see. The philosophical implications and applicability of such imagery is not difficult to discern, not least because they reflect one of the prevailing and recurring philosophical motifs in Shakespeare's work, viz., the conflict between realism and nominalism or relativism.[1] In these words of Juliet, and indeed throughout the entirety of the play, the imagery of night versus day is a signifier for the conflict between nominalism and realism. In seeing or desiring no reality beyond the beauty in each other's eyes, the lovers have spurned objective reality in favor of subjective experience. The day, with its hustle and bustle of other people demanding interaction, is too objectively real for the lovers. They desire each other, and resent the interjection of others, of reality, of the objective truth beyond the self. Thus, says Juliet, "if love be blind, / It best agrees with night". Their love does not bring them light but blindness. If everyone loved as

---

[1] In *Hamlet*, for instance, this philosophical conflict could be said to constitute the play's very raison d'être.

Juliet loved, "all the world [would] be in love with night" and would "pay no worship to the garish sun". We would all be collectively in the darkness of our own self-referential passions and would pay no heed to the light of an undesired and intrusive reality.

The consequences of such subjectivism are exhibited in the extremes of passion to which Juliet is subject when she learns of Romeo's slaying of Tybalt. At first, her anger and venom are directed against Romeo:

> O serpent heart, hid with a flow'ring face!
> Did ever dragon keep so fair a cave?
> Beautiful tyrant! fiend angelical!
> Dove-feather'd raven! wolvish-ravening lamb!
> Despised substance of divinest show!
> Just opposite to what thou justly seem'st,
> A damned saint, an honourable villain!
> O nature, what hadst thou to do in hell,
> When thou didst bower the spirit of a fiend
> In mortal paradise of such sweet flesh?
> Was ever book containing such vile matter
> So fairly bound? O, that deceit should dwell
> In such a gorgeous palace!
>
> (3.2.73–84)

Her words are replete with satanic imagery ("serpent", "dragon", "fiend", "damned", "hell"), but their overall tenor is directed at the dichotomy between that which truly *is* and that which only *seems to be*.

The truth is not what it seems: Romeo's "serpent heart" is concealed by his "flow'ring face"; the "spirit of a fiend" is clothed in "such sweet flesh"; the "fairly bound" book contains "such vile matter"; "deceit" dwells in "such a gorgeous palace". Romeo is a "beautiful tyrant" and a "fiend angelical"—*truly* a tyrant who *seemed* to be beautiful, *truly* a fiend who *seemed* to be angelic. He is *truly* a raven who *seemed* to be a dove; *truly* a ravenous wolf who *seemed* to be a lamb; *truly* damned who *seemed* to be a saint; *truly* a villain who *seemed* to be honorable. In all these ways he is just the opposite of what he "justly seem'st". The ugliness of his evil is disguised by the beauty of his mask. And lest we miss the philosophical ramifications of this dichotomy, Shakespeare places a specifically philosophical reference in the very midst of the invective: Romeo's *substance* is despicable in spite of its "divinest show". He is *truly* despicable even if he *seemed* to be godlike.

The philosophical undercurrent of Juliet's despair-driven words reminds us insistently of the philosophical conundrum at the heart of *Hamlet*. "Seems, madam!" exclaims Hamlet. "Nay, it is; I know not seems" (1.2.76). In these words to his mother and in those that follow, Hamlet exhibits a deep understanding of metaphysics, echoing Aristotle and Saint Thomas Aquinas in their distinction between the *substance* or *essence* of things and their *accidental* qualities, between that which is and that which only seems to be. There is, however, a huge difference between the truth-seeking Hamlet and the passion-driven Juliet. Hamlet tells us that he has "that within which passes show" (1.2.85) whereas Juliet, in spite of this brief outburst against her lover, is continually dazzled by the mere "show" of things so that she has difficulty distinguishing reality from fantasy, or virtue from vice. Let's not forget that she barely knows Romeo, having met him briefly on only three occasions, during which they had waxed lyrical in the besotted idolization of each other. The fact is that she had fallen for his "flow'ring face" and his "sweet flesh", his accidental qualities, the "divinest show", without ever inquiring about the deepest substance that dwells within. Preferring the fogginess of feeling to the clarity of vision, she shrouds herself in the mists of misperception, blinded by a love that "best agrees with night" and spurns the day. It is, therefore, no surprise that she lurches from one extreme of passion to the other, abandoning her initial disdain for Romeo for a renewal of her idolatry. Thus, when the Nurse concurs with her disdainful attack on him, she instantly leaps to his defense:

> Blister'd be thy tongue
> For such a wish! He was not born to shame:
> Upon his brow shame is asham'd to sit;
> For 'tis a throne where honour may be crown'd
> Sole monarch of the universal earth.
> O, what a beast was I to chide at him!
>   (3.2.90–95)

As usual, her passion-driven words are utterly heedless and careless of the facts. She does not seek to know the details of the duel. She does not ask whether Romeo or Tybalt had initiated the argument, or which party was to blame for provoking the other. Such facts are unimportant. She knows that Romeo, whom she scarcely knows at all, is perfect. His actions cannot be shameful because shame itself is ashamed to sit on his blameless brow. Indeed, his brow is the very throne upon which honor is crowned. Coming so soon after her vitriolic invective, this display of veneration, this volteface, is farcical. Far from being the "serpent", "dragon", and "fiend", who is "damned", Romeo is now elevated to the level of the very gods, his brow crowned with the honor upon which honor itself is crowned the "sole monarch of the universal earth". Thus Juliet blinds herself with the "divinest show", worshipping her false god, her fantasy, forsaking that which truly is for that which merely seems to be.

10

"HEAVEN IS HERE WHERE JULIET LIVES"

Having waxed idolatrous about Romeo, Juliet laments his banishment, proclaiming that the one word " 'banished' . . . hath slain ten thousand Tybalts" (3.2.113–14). She then appears to express a desire for death, and perhaps even a determination to commit suicide: "I'll to my wedding-bed, / And death, not Romeo, take my maiden-head!" (3.2.136–37). In the following scene, Romeo responds to the news of his banishment in much the same way as had Juliet:

> There is no world without Verona walls,
> But purgatory, torture, hell itself.
> Hence banished is banish'd from the world,
> And world's exile is death. Then "banished"
> Is death mis-term'd; calling death "banished",
> Thou cut'st my head off with a golden axe,
> And smilest upon the stroke that murders me.
>
> (3.3.17–23)

Condemning this response as a "deadly sin" and a "rude unthankfulness" (3.3.24), Friar Lawrence sees Romeo's lack of gratitude to be indicative of a lack of humility and, therefore, a mortal sin. Since the law demanded death for Romeo's crime, the Prince had shown great clemency in sentencing him to exile. "This is dear mercy," exclaims the Friar, "and thou seest it not" (3.3.28). In juxtaposing a justice that demands death and a mercy that transmutes the death sentence to mere exile, Shakespeare's Christian audience would have seen the connection between the justice and mercy of God, the former of which is always mitigated by the latter. The original sinners, Adam and Eve, deserved death for their act of primal disobedience, yet God's mercy, taking precedence over justice, transmuted the sentence to one of banishment or exile. In similar fashion, Romeo, as a child of Adam, deserves death for his sin but is granted banishment instead. Allegorically the Prince serves as an *alter Christus*, bestowing mercy in the place of justice, whereas Romeo serves as an Everyman figure, representing each of us in our sins. It is, therefore, no surprise that Romeo's anger at the Prince's mercy is seen by the shocked Friar as a "deadly sin". It is indeed a "rude unthankfulness" to shun the mercy of God, even if that providential mercy is shown to us via a third party.

The fact that the whole question of justice and mercy was at the forefront of Shakespeare's mind when he was writing *Romeo and Juliet* can be seen from its prominent place in *The Merchant of Venice*, a play he wrote at around the same time. Portia's famous "quality of mercy" speech is rightly celebrated as one of the highlights of *The Merchant of Venice* and, indeed, one of the highlights of the entire Shakespearean canon. Mercy, Portia tells us, is a gift of grace, "an attribute to God himself" (4.1.195), that "droppeth as the gentle rain from heaven" (4.1.185). Mercy is also inseparable from gratitude, as is signified by their linguistic unity in modern French, in which *merci* means "mercy" but also "thank you". Ingratitude in the face of mercy in such a grave matter is, therefore, a mortal sin, a "rude unthankfulness". Friar Lawrence is right, and we should bear this in mind as we look closer at Romeo's plaintive response to the news of his banishment.

The theological dimension at the heart of Romeo's ungrateful response to the Prince's mercy is evident in his conflation of purgatory, torture, and hell. From a Catholic perspective, and let's not forget that Romeo and the Friar are Catholics, as is Shakespeare, the conflation of purgatory and hell is tantamount to blasphemy. Those in purgatory are saved, whereas those in hell are damned. Purgatory can be seen as an antechamber of heaven, the place where sins are purged; it is the blessed place where repentant sinners are showered with God's merciful love, their sins being washed away with penitential tears. It is the very place where mercy trumps justice. Romeo does not desire mercy, and he fails to distinguish between purgatory and hell because he has no penitential tears to shed. There are no tears of sorrow for his actions, nor are there any tears for the deceased Tybalt or Mercutio. He only has tears for himself, tears of self-pity. It is no wonder that the Friar condemns his ingratitude as a mortal sin.

The reason that Romeo is heedless of the four last things (death, judgment, heaven, and hell) is that he is heedless of anything and everything except his idolatrous obsession with Juliet. "There is no world without Verona walls" because there is no world, either in this mortal life or in eternity, that he desires beyond his possession of Juliet. And this is the real heart of the tragedy, the paradoxical and ironic twist whereby Romeo and Juliet are possessed by their possession of each other, driven to madness by an obsessive and possessive "love" that excludes any other love and which exorcises both God and neighbor from their affections. The awful lesson that *Romeo and Juliet* teaches is that the thing possessed possesses the possessor. This is seen in Romeo's next blasphemous remark in which he exclaims that "heaven is here / Where Juliet lives" (3.3.29–30). Juliet is Romeo's alpha and omega, his beginning and end. She is the goddess to which he owes the sum of all his worship. Heaven is where Juliet lives because Juliet is his deity. He would choose this "heaven" even when it becomes his hell.

Although one is reminded perhaps of the similarly obsessive love between Heathcliff and Catherine in Emily Brontë's *Wuthering Heights*, it is difficult to read these lines without the powerful image of Dante's Paolo and Francesca emerging once more from the allegorical shadows. Blown hither and thither by the heedless winds of sexual passion,[1] the sin of Dante's damned lovers parallels that of Shakespeare's Romeo and Juliet:

> The souls condemned to bear these punishments,
> I learned, are the carnal sinners, of lust so strong
> that they let it master reason and good sense.[2]

In another translation of these lines the lustful are condemned as "those who make reason slave to appetite",[3] and this is the root of Romeo's problem. He and Juliet have overthrown reason and good sense in pursuit of their passion. In so doing, they have made reason the slave of the irrational, subservient to the force of feeling and the sway of emotion. Shakespeare, like Dante, is steeped in

[1] "In wide and clustering flocks wing-borne, wind-borne / Even so they go, the souls who did this treason, / Hither and thither, and up and down, outworn, / Hopeless of any rest . . .". Dante, *Inferno*, canto 5, lines 41–44, in *The Divine Comedy, Part 1: Hell*, trans. Dorothy L. Sayers (London: Penguin Classics, 1949), p. 98.

[2] Dante, *Inferno*, canto 5, lines 37–39, trans. Michael Palma, Norton Critical Edition (New York: W. W. Norton, 2008), p. 19.

[3] Dante, *Inferno*, canto 5, lines 37–39, trans. Mark Musa (New York: Penguin Classics, 2003), p. 110.

the scholastic philosophy of Saint Thomas Aquinas. He knows that reason must never be abandoned. Love, like faith, must be subject to reason; a love that denies or defies reason is illicit and is not really love at all, at least not in its fullest and truest sense.

Romeo, on the other hand, is profoundly irrational, spurning philosophy and elevating feeling above all else. This is evident in his anti-philosophical response to Friar Lawrence's attempts to reason with him:

> *Friar Lawrence.* Thou fond mad man, hear me a little speak.
> *Romeo.* O, thou wilt speak again of banishment.
> *Friar Lawrence.* I'll give thee armour to keep off that word;
>   Adversity's sweet milk, philosophy,
>   To comfort thee, though thou art banished.
> *Romeo.* Yet "banished"? Hang up philosophy;
>   Unless philosophy can make a Juliet,
>   Displant a town, reverse a prince's doom,
>   It helps not, it prevails not. Talk no more.
> *Friar Lawrence.* O, then I see that madmen have no ears.
> *Romeo.* How should they, when that wise men have no eyes?
> *Friar Lawrence.* Let me dispute with thee of thy estate.
> *Romeo.* Thou canst not speak of that thou dost not feel.
>   Wert thou as young as I, Juliet thy love,
>   An hour but married, Tybalt murdered,
>   Doting like me, and like me banished,
>   Then mightst thou speak, then mightst thou tear thy hair,
>   And fall upon the ground, as I do now,
>   Taking the measure of an unmade grave.
>
> (3.3.52–70)

In this exchange, Romeo emerges as an anti-Boethius, as one who refuses to be consoled by philosophy. Yet he is worse than this. He not only fails to be comforted by philosophy; he refuses even to acknowledge that philosophy has any purpose whatsoever. His crime against reason is not merely one of obstinacy but of obfuscation. Like Juliet, he prefers the darkness of his moods and his passion to the light of reason and truth. Philosophy can be hanged, as far as he is concerned, unless it can give him what he wants. Unless it can deliver Juliet to him and remove all obstacles to their union, he has no use for it. Since heaven is defined by Juliet's presence, philosophy can go to hell.

Not surprisingly, Friar Lawrence is once more alarmed by Romeo's response. Whereas the earlier failure to greet mercy with gratitude, with its consequent failure to discern the fundamental difference between purgatory and hell, was a sin against theological orthodoxy, this latest response by Romeo is a crime against philosophical realism. Such a defiance of reason marks Romeo, in the Friar's eyes, as one of the "madmen". The madness, as Romeo reveals when Friar Lawrence tries again to "dispute" with him about his condition, is the madness of relativism:

> Thou canst not speak of that thou dost not feel.
> Wert thou as young as I, Juliet thy love,
> An hour but married, Tybalt murdered,
> Doting like me, and like me banished,
> Then mightst thou speak.
>
> (3.3.64–68)

Romeo's riposte is the relativist position stripped of all sophistry. He asserts that his own feelings are the only judge of reality, and that personal experiences and feelings are the only real truth. And since there is no truth beyond ourselves and our feelings, there is no other truth that can speak to us with any authority. "Truth" is about us and what we feel. Romeo tells the philosopher who is trying to reason with him that he can only speak the truth if he felt what

Romeo feels, if he were as young as Romeo, if he loved Juliet, if he had been married for only an hour, if he had murdered Tybalt, if he were in love, and if he were banished from Verona. In short, and to put the matter bluntly, the philosopher could only teach Romeo anything if he were in fact Romeo! There is indeed no reasoning with such "madness", and we are not surprised that Romeo ends his impassioned dismissal of philosophical realism by tearing his hair, falling on the ground, and wishing he were dead. In Romeo's case, relativism leads to nihilism, and self-centeredness to thoughts of suicide.

"Take heed, take heed, for such die miserable", warns the Friar (3.3.145). Yet Romeo is heedless because he is headless, losing his head in his loss of reason. Like Paolo and Francesca he had made his reason the slave of his feelings, losing his head as surely as he had lost his heart. Desiring neither faith nor reason, and believing in nothing beyond the "heaven" of Juliet's presence, Romeo somnambulates heedlessly and headlessly toward a hell of his own devising.

"O MISCHIEF, THOU ART SWIFT"

Much of the dramatic dynamism of *Romeo and Juliet* is a consequence of the indecent haste and rashness with which the protagonists conduct themselves and the way in which this unseemly haste impacts their relationships with others. It is the lack of virtue, and particularly the lack of the cardinal virtues of prudence and temperance, which drives the plot forward with such ultimately destructive force. It is as though the hastiness and rashness of the individual characters accelerates events until every one of them is swept up into a maelstrom to which they have each contributed a small but significant part. In the final reckoning, as we survey the debris following the debacle that is the play's denouement, it seems that each character has reaped the destructive harvest of the sins that he has sown

At the play's tragic heart is the rashness and hastiness of the lovers themselves. As they hurtle headlong into each other's arms, heedless of the many obstacles and hurdles that should have given them pause for prudential thought and cause for tempered passion, Romeo and Juliet set themselves on a collision course with calamity. Yet they are not the only culprits. Indeed, their plight is worsened and their doom is hastened by the hastiness of others. The Friar's failure to adhere to the tenets of Christian moderation that he urges on the lovers, and his willingness to marry them so soon after their first meeting and without the knowledge or consent of their parents, contributes greatly to the unfolding catastrophe. The inability of Mercutio and Tybalt to temper their anger leads to their respective deaths, and Romeo's inability to temper his own anger leads to his banishment. Yet it is the rashness and hastiness of the older generation that fuels the flames of passion. It is the feud between the two families that fuels the violence that leads to Mercutio's and Tybalt's deaths, and Romeo's exile, and it is this self-same feud that necessitates the secrecy of the lovers and the clandestine nature of their actions. In a more general sense, we can deduce that the hot-headedness and hot-bloodedness of Romeo and Juliet, their rashness and impetuosity, and their lack of Christian virtue, have been learned from their parents. To put the matter simply, it is the sins of the parents that are largely responsible for the deaths of their children.

Nowhere are the destructive consequences of poor parenting more apparent than in Capulet's decision to force Juliet into a hasty marriage to Paris. We will recall that Capulet had initially resisted Paris' suit on the grounds that Juliet was too young to marry:

> My child is yet a stranger in the world,
> She hath not seen the change of fourteen years;
> Let two more summers wither in their pride
> Ere we may think her ripe to be a bride.
>
> (1.2.8–11)

When Paris complained that girls younger than Juliet "are happy mothers made" (1.2.12), Capulet's response had been unequivocal: "And too soon marr'd are those so early made" (1.2.13). It seems, at this stage, that Capulet is a prudent father who wishes Juliet to be at least sixteen before she is married, fearing that an early marriage would be harmful to his daughter's health. And yet, astonishingly, on the very next day, he changes his mind. Worse, he decides that his daughter shall be married to Paris almost immediately, i.e., two days later. Realizing that a marriage in the family might seem inappropriate so soon after the slaying of his kinsman Tybalt, he decides to postpone the wedding, but only by one extra day! Thus, on the very day that Tybalt is killed, and on the day after he had declared that it would be a further two years before his daughter was old enough to marry, Capulet decides that the wedding should take place three days hence. Aware that such undue haste might seem indecent so soon after Tybalt's death, he declares that the wedding must not be accompanied by too much unseemly revelry:

> We'll keep no great ado—a friend or two;
> For, hark you, Tybalt being slain so late,
> It may be thought we held him carelessly,
> Being our kinsman, if we revel much;
> Therefore we'll have some half a dozen friends,
> And there an end.
>
> (3.4.23–28)

The rashness and impetuosity of Capulet is such that the size of the party is already increasing even as he speaks. He begins with plans for "a friend or two" and, four lines later, speaks of "some half a dozen friends". Needless to say, by the following morning, he is making plans for a full-scale celebration with a burgeoning guest list. Meanwhile, his daughter, exhibiting the same sort of disastrous impetuosity and rashness, had already married in undue haste and was spending her first (and last) night with her new husband. It

is, therefore, ironic that Juliet should complain of the hastiness of her father's plan. "I wonder at this haste" (3.5.118),
she tells her mother when she learns of the impending
marriage. Refusing to comply with her father's wishes, she
earns the disdain of her mother, who wishes "the fool were
married to her grave" (3.5.140), and the outright fury of
her father. Falling to her knees, Juliet begs leave to explain
herself:

> Good father, I beseech you on my knees,
> Hear me with patience but to speak a word.
>
> (3.5.159)

Not known for his patience, Capulet silences his daughter
with a litany of abuse:

> Hang thee, young baggage! disobedient wretch!
> I tell thee what—get thee to church a Thursday,
> Or never after look me in the face.
> Speak not, reply not, do not answer me;
> My fingers itch. Wife, we scarce thought us blest
> That God had lent us but this only child;
> But now I see this one is one too much,
> And that we have a curse in having her.
> Out on her, hilding!
>
> (3.5.160–68)

The tempestuous intemperance exhibited in his anger is
akin to the fatal distemper that cost Tybalt and Mercutio
their lives and Romeo his freedom to live in Verona. And,
indeed, Capulet's intemperance will prove as deadly as theirs,
though it will be his daughter's death and not his own that
is its consequence. Juliet is reduced to cowering silence by
her father's rage ("Speak not, reply not, do not answer me"),
and in her enforced silence any prospect or possibility of a

full confession that might have averted the tragedy is lost. We should note also that Capulet's words are as full of the blameworthy ingratitude that had characterized Romeo's earlier shunning of the Prince's mercy. He laments that their only child was not a blessing or a gift from God but "a curse". Such ingratitude, as the Friar would no doubt have told him had he been present, constituted a "deadly sin" and a "rude unthankfulness". Such sins are indeed deadly and such unthankfulness worthy of rebuke. It would take the death of his daughter to teach Capulet that he was partially to blame for the tragedy. Her death was his own sins' self-inflicted punishment.

As Juliet is on her knees at her father's feet, no doubt weeping inconsolably, she finds an unlikely champion in the Nurse. "God in heaven bless her!" the Nurse exclaims. "You are to blame, my lord, to rate her so" (3.5.169). The Nurse shows great courage in daring to speak out in the midst of the ire of an irascible rogue such as Capulet, and her words carry considerable moral weight. In the face of Capulet's consideration of Juliet as a "curse", the Nurse's call for "God in heaven" to "bless her" serves as a potent rebuke. Like all children, Juliet is a blessing to her parents, and their failure to appreciate such a blessing is the real curse that afflicts the family. It is not that Juliet is a curse but that she is herself cursed by parents who fail to see her as a blessing. In this light, the Nurse's insistence that Capulet is "to blame" has far-ranging ramifications well beyond his present blameworthiness in berating his daughter so. He is to blame for the way that he has raised her; in the example of self-centered impetuosity that he has set her; in the lack of love that he has shown her; in his lack of gratitude for her. And it is Juliet's curse to have been shaped by this example. Her own acts of impulsiveness, her lack of love for her parents, her lack of gratitude, are the consequences of the example she has been set by her parents. It is their curse, and hers, that the bad example that they have set for their daughter will contribute to her downfall and their bereavement.

The double entendre implicit in the Nurse's rebuke to Capulet is also noteworthy. Capulet is to blame in the way he *rates* Juliet in both senses of the word "rate", i.e., to scold and to judge. He is to blame both for scolding her so angrily and for judging her value in such negative terms. He is too hasty in berating her as well as in debasing her true worth. Even more striking is the double entendre implicit in the literal sarcasm of Capulet's response to the Nurse's interjection and the allegorical irony with which Shakespeare invests it:

> And why, my Lady Wisdom? Hold your tongue,
> Good Prudence; smatter with your gossips, go.
>
> (3.5.170–71)

On the literal level, Capulet is simply sneering at the sheer chutzpah of the Nurse, a mere servant, in daring to offer counsel to her master; on the allegorical level, however, the Nurse is, in this one instant, the voice of wisdom and of prudence. It is, therefore, deeply ironic that Capulet should tell "wisdom" to hold her tongue, and "prudence" to be gone from his presence. Lacking these virtuous attributes and desiring to be free from their constraints, he proceeds on a path of recklessness, abandoning reason in favor of the selfish demands of his own desires. Too myopic to see the consequences of his actions, Capulet in his reckless abandon will prompt his daughter to abandon herself to recklessness.

Considering Shakespeare's employment of ironic allegory in these preceding words, it is tempting to see similar irony in Capulet's further dismissal of the Nurse's continuing efforts to speak:

> Peace, you mumbling fool!
> Utter your gravity o'er a gossip's bowl,
> For here we need it not.
>
> (3.5.173–74)

If "wisdom" is to hold her tongue, and prudence is told to "go", it is easy to see an ironic intent in Capulet's dismissal of "peace" as a "mumbling fool". The Nurse can utter her "gravity", i.e., her serious advice, elsewhere, "for here we need it not". Capulet is exercising his authority to exorcise all words of wisdom from his presence, and, in so doing, is silencing those who might have enlightened him about the gravity of the situation in the light of Juliet's marriage to Romeo. Whether Juliet might have confessed or whether the Nurse might have confided the secret to Capulet, they are prevented from doing so by Capulet's own threats and rantings. His blustering keeps him impregnably ignorant, and the ensuing silence is not only deathly but deadly.

With daughter and nurse kowtowed, Capulet ends his rant with a threat to disown his daughter if she refuses to marry Paris and to throw her onto the streets to starve:

> ... hang, beg, starve, die in the streets,
> For, by my soul, I'll ne'er acknowledge thee,
> Nor what is mine shall never do thee good.
> Trust to't; bethink you; I'll not be forsworn.
>
> (3.5.193–96)

As Capulet storms off, his threats ringing in our ears, we feel sympathy for Juliet's plight as never before, a sympathy

that is heightened by the utter pathos of her pleading to
her mother:

> Is there no pity sitting in the clouds
> That sees into the bottom of my grief?
> O, sweet my mother, cast me not away!
> Delay this marriage for a month, a week;
> Or, if you do not, make the bridal bed
> In that dim monument where Tybalt lies.
>
> (3.5.197–202)

The depths of her despair, the pathetic pleading for a mother's
love and support, and the portentous evocation, pregnant
with prophecy, of the tomb where Tybalt lies, all combine
to elicit our sympathy for the plight of this hapless thirteen-
year-old girl. The parent in each of us pleads on her behalf,
much as the Chorus in a Greek tragedy pleads with the
protagonist for justice or clemency, but all to no avail. Lady
Capulet is as heartless and as unfeeling as her husband, and,
like her husband, silences the girl before she can speak,
thereby thwarting any possibility of a revelation of Juliet's
marriage to Romeo:

> Talk not to me, for I'll not speak a word;
> Do as thou wilt, for I have done with thee.
>
> (3.5.203–4)

Having disowned her daughter as heartlessly as had her
husband, Lady Capulet walks out on the weeping girl. This
is the high point of our sympathy for Juliet. Bereft of a
mother's and father's love, she is left in a seemingly hopeless situation with nobody but the Nurse for support:

> O God!—O nurse! how shall this be prevented?
> My husband is on earth, my faith in heaven;

How shall that faith return again to earth,
Unless that husband send it me from heaven
By leaving earth? Comfort me, counsel me.
Alack, alack, that heaven should practise stratagems
Upon so soft a subject as myself!
What say'st thou! Hast thou not a word of joy?
Some comfort, nurse.

$$(3.5.205-13)$$

If we feel sympathy for Juliet's distress and for the increasingly difficult situation in which she finds herself, it is much more difficult to sympathize with the idolatrous heterodoxy of her words. Her faith has deserted her; it is "in heaven" and beyond her earthly reach. She only has faith in Romeo, who, as the god of her new faith, is the only one able to administer grace to her pining and repining soul. Her faith can only return again if Romeo sends it to her from heaven. Nobody but Romeo has this power over her soul, not even God himself. It seems indeed that God has become her adversary, practicing stratagems upon her, setting traps for her soul. Such heavenly intervention is, in Juliet's estimation, neither wanted nor warranted. Entirely absent from her plaintive expostulation is any sense of responsibility or culpability for her own actions, the negative consequences of which are seen as traps set by heaven. Placing all her faith in Romeo, she wishes to ignore God when things are going well, subsuming her conscience to her desire, and to blame him when things go wrong, considering the consequences of her choices as a heavenly conspiracy against her.

Finding no comfort in heaven, Juliet turns to the Nurse for "comfort" and "joy". She is disappointed. The Nurse advises her to forget about her marriage to Romeo and to marry Paris as her parents wish. In the Nurse's eyes, Romeo

is but a "dishclout" (3.5.220) beside the handsome Paris and
that, in any case, Romeo's banishment means he's as good as
dead. After the Nurse departs, Juliet curses her and resolves
never to confide in her again. Forcibly separated from Romeo
and deserted by her parents and by her only confidante, Juliet
turns to Friar Lawrence, the only person whom she can trust:

> I'll to the friar to know his remedy;
> If all else fail, myself have power to die.
>
> (3.5.242–43)

Juliet's ominous death wish at the conclusion of act 3
sets the scene for the beginning of the following act in
which her thoughts and threats of suicide abound. Lament-
ing to Friar Lawrence that she is "past hope, past cure,
past help" (4.1.45), she shows him the knife with which
she will kill herself unless the Friar can prevent her impending marriage to Paris:

> Therefore, out of thy long-experience'd time,
> Give me some present counsel; or, behold,
> 'Twixt my extremes and me this bloody knife
> Shall play the umpire, arbitrating that
> Which the commission of thy years and art
> Could to no issue of true honour bring.
> Be not so long to speak; I long to die,
> If what thou speak'st speak not of remedy.
>
> (4.1.60–67)

Faced with such a deadly ultimatum, the Friar concocts

> a kind of hope,
> Which craves as desperate an execution
> As that is desperate which we would prevent.
>
> (4.1.68–70)

Holding out a vial of "distilled liquor" (4.1.94) which has the power to simulate death in the one who takes it, the Friar counsels Juliet to take it, promising her that he and Romeo will be waiting for her when she revives, after which Romeo will take her with him to Mantua. Thus is set in motion the final comedy of errors that will lead to the culminating tragedy.

Should the Friar have offered such "desperate" counsel to such a desperate girl? Is he somehow culpable for her death in so doing? These questions continue to divide the critics. What, one wonders, were his options? Considering the apparent determination of Juliet to take her own life, and her own insistence that only the Friar's counsel could stay her hand, it is clear that the Friar needed to take some action to prevent the distraught girl's death. One option might have been the Friar's candid confession to Capulet that he had already presided over the marriage of Juliet to Romeo, thereby rendering Juliet's marriage to Paris impossible. Bearing in mind Capulet's frightening display of anger when Juliet had refused to marry Paris, one can only guess at the apoplexy that would have accompanied the revelation that his daughter had secretly married the son of his sworn enemy! Perhaps the prospect of such an apoplectic apocalypse was too much for either Juliet or the Friar to contemplate. The other alternative would have been for the Friar to smuggle Juliet to Mantua, reuniting her with her exiled husband. This surely would have been a less perilous course of action than that which the Friar actually counseled. On the other hand, it is possible that the Friar might have forfeited his own life or freedom if he were found to be complicit in Juliet's removal to Mantua. Did fear prevent him from suggesting such an escape? And why, one wonders, did Juliet not suggest such an escape

herself? After all, none of the dangers inherent in the journey to Mantua could equal the certain death inherent in
her proposed suicide.

Perhaps such earnest questioning of the plot, and of the
motives of the plotters, is somewhat self-defeating. Shakespeare was merely following the well-worn plot of the source
from which he drew his inspiration, one which demanded
the simulated death and the double suicide. If the mech-
anism by which the plot is followed and the denouement
achieved is somewhat contrived, shouldn't we blame the
constraints of the source rather than the lack of ingenuity
in Shakespeare's adaptation? On the other hand, is it not
legitimate to see in such incongruity a genuine deficiency
in both the source and the adaptation? Or, alternatively,
should we simply agree to suspend our disbelief in conformity to the formal demands of tragedy itself? Should
we simply refrain from asking such awkward questions in
deference to the generic limitations of the genre? To put
the matter in the vulgarity of the vernacular, shouldn't we
cut Shakespeare some slack? In any event, and to put a
merciful end to such speculations, it is at least clear that
the Friar is motivated in his desperate plan by the desperate extremity of the situation in which he and Juliet find
themselves, a desperate situation for which they are both
culpable in the sense that the marriage to Romeo was rash
and ill-advised.

There is also one other mitigating factor in Friar Lawrence's
defense, and one which is all too often overlooked. The Friar's
scheme is judged by the critics with the wisdom of hindsight, in their privileged foreknowledge that the scheme will
end tragically. The Friar is therefore condemned for putting
Juliet in such a *potentially* fatal situation. We should remember, however, that Juliet was already in an *imminently* fatal

situation (her threatened suicide) when the Friar suggested the scheme. We should also remember that neither the Friar nor Juliet is privileged with knowledge of the future. Neither of them seems to have considered the scheme potentially fatal, as is apparent from the fact that the prospect of mortal danger is not a part of their dialogue on the subject. Nowhere is it suggested that the Friar's concoction is potentially harmful, and the Friar is clearly proceeding in absolute confidence that the concoction will work in the way that he describes. And indeed it *does* work exactly as he describes. Without the wisdom of hindsight, we have to concede that the scheme might have worked and, indeed, we have to assume, with the Friar, that it would have worked. Indeed, it *should* have worked if it had not been for several unforeseen and unforeseeable twists of fate, or providence, for which the Friar can hardly be considered culpable.

The first unforeseen twist is Capulet's decision to bring the wedding between Juliet and Paris forward a day from Thursday to Wednesday, i.e., to the following day, contradicting his own judgment of the previous day that "Wednesday is too soon" (3.4.19). As is so often the case throughout the play, undue haste and rashness of judgment bring disastrous consequences. In this case, Capulet's impetuosity will cost his daughter her life. In bringing the wedding forward, Capulet forces Juliet to take the sleeping potion a day earlier, thereby accelerating the action beyond the control of Friar Lawrence's best-laid schemes. When Friar John, who is entrusted by Friar Lawrence to deliver the message to Romeo in Mantua, is unavoidably detained (another unforeseen twist), the fate of Juliet is sealed. By the time that Friar Lawrence learns that the message had not been delivered, Romeo had already received news of Juliet's "death" from his servant Balthasar. If, however, Capulet had not brought the wedding forward a day, Juliet would not have taken the potion a day early, and Balthasar would not have rushed to Mantua to deliver the fateful and fatal news. Furthermore, Friar John's detention would not have mattered because he would still have had time to get word to Romeo before the latter received news from anyone else. In short, and in sum, Capulet's lack of prudence or temperance will play a crucial role in the death of his daughter.

It seems that there is no escaping the moral motif that Shakespeare places at the play's racing heart. A lack of virtue leads to a lack of judgment, and, specifically, intemperance and imprudence hasten the downfall of those who refuse to temper their passions. This theme is played out once again with the undue haste with which Romeo acts upon hearing news of Juliet's "death". Indeed, his desperate response prompts Balthasar to urge restraint:

> I do beseech you, sir, have patience;
> Your looks are pale and wild, and do import
> Some misadventure.
>
> (5.1.27–29)

Having reassured Balthasar that he is "deceived" and that his fears and forebodings are unjustified, Romeo sends him away to hire horses for their immediate return to Verona. As soon as Balthasar has departed, Romeo's thoughts turn to suicide:

> Well, Juliet, I will lie with thee to-night.
> Let's see for means. O mischief, thou art swift
> To enter in the thoughts of desperate men!
>
> (5.1.34–35)

Lacking the patience that Balthasar urged, Romeo succumbs to the "mischief" and rashness of unbridled passion.

In doing so, he is following the destructive pattern of so many of the play's protagonists. Mischief is indeed swift to enter the thoughts and govern the actions of those who refuse to be governed by reason and virtue. In this context, the "mischief" of which Romeo speaks is supernaturally evil and not merely generically "harmful". As in the phrase "where the mischief have you been?",[1] in which "mischief" is a synonym for the devil himself, the mischief that enters so swiftly into the thoughts of the sinfully passionate is akin to demonic possession, as though the vacuum created by virtue's absence is filled swiftly with the venality of vice. Such mischief is a maelstrom that leaves a path of destruction in its wake. Having already claimed the lives of Mercutio and Tybalt, the mischief entering so swiftly into Romeo's thoughts will soon lead to the deaths of Juliet and Paris, as well as Romeo himself.

[1] Although this phrase is seldom used today, it was common enough in the nineteenth century and features in the works of Henry James and Rudyard Kipling among others.

"THIS SIGHT OF DEATH IS AS A BELL"

O my love! my wife!
Death, that hath suck'd the honey of thy breath,
Hath had no power yet upon thy beauty.
Thou art not conquer'd; beauty's ensign yet
Is crimson in thy lips and in thy cheeks,
And death's pale flag is not advanced there.
                                        (5.3.91–96)

As Romeo arrives at Juliet's tomb, killing the hapless Paris en route, he is shocked that Juliet's face does not resemble that of a corpse. Although she had "died" more than twenty-four hours earlier, he is surprised that death appears to have no power over her beauty. Indeed, her lips and cheeks are red, indicating the presence of life. Anyone who had ever seen a corpse within an hour of death, or anyone with a rudimentary knowledge of medicine, would have been startled and perhaps even horrified at the clear presence of a living body in the tomb. Romeo is, however, blind to the life before him and the "resurrection" that is about to occur. Whether this is a further example of an incongruity in the plot or whether, suspending our disbelief, we accept Romeo's singular blindness, the fact is that he does not have eyes for the "miracle" about to unfold before him. Instead, he is merely puzzled by Juliet's beauty and employs a superstitious and non-Christian metaphor to illustrate his horror at the presence of death:

> Ah, dear Juliet,
> Why art thou yet so fair? Shall I believe
> That unsubstantial Death is amorous,
> And that the lean abhorred monster keeps
> Thee here in dark to be his paramour?
>
> (5.3.101–5)

Yet, as Romeo prepares to take the poison that will end his life, his thoughts are heedless of the eternal consequences of the action he is about take. Narcissistically fixated with his own suffering and necrophilically transfixed by the reclining Juliet, he pays no attention to death's connection to judgment, or to the soul's eternal destiny in either heaven or hell. In stark contrast, it was the knowledge of these ultimate realities that had stayed Hamlet's hand when he too had considered suicide as an option:

> O, that this too too solid flesh would melt,
> Thaw, and resolve itself into a dew!
> Or that the Everlasting had not fix'd
> His canon 'gainst self-slaughter! O God! God!
> How weary, stale, flat, and unprofitable,
> Seem to me all the uses of this world!
>
> (Hamlet, 1.2.129–34)

Hamlet, as a conscientious Christian, desired death as desperately as Romeo, but, unlike Romeo, his thoughts and actions are usually characterized by a patient circumspection born of prudence and temperance. It is his awareness that God, "the Everlasting", had "fix'd His canon 'gainst self-slaughter" that prevents him from taking his own life.

Similarly, in his famous soliloquy, Hamlet ponders the four last things (death, judgment, heaven, and hell) as he once again dallies with the desire to end his life:

> To die: to sleep—
> No more; and by a sleep to say we end
> The heart-ache and the thousand natural shocks
> That flesh is heir to. 'Tis a consummation
> Devoutly to be wish'd. To die, to sleep;
> To sleep, perchance to dream. Ay, there's the rub;
> For in that sleep of death what dreams may come,
> When we have shuffled off this mortal coil,
> Must give us pause. There's the respect
> That makes calamity of so long life;
> For who would bear the whips and scorns of time,
> Th' oppressor's wrong, the proud man's contumely,
> The pangs of despis'd love, the law's delay,
> The insolence of office, and the spurns
> That patient merit of th' unworthy takes,
> When he himself might his quietus make
> With a bare bodkin? Who would fardels bear,
> To grunt and sweat under a weary life,
> But that the dread of something after death—
> The undiscover'd country, from whose bourn
> No traveller returns—puzzles the will,
> And makes us rather bear those ills we have
> Than fly to others that we know not of?
>
> (*Hamlet*, 3.1.60–82)

Hamlet's awareness of the mortally sinful nature of suicide gives him pause for thought as he ponders the consequences of taking his own life. If a suicidal death is the final defiant sin against life and its God, if it is the final acceptance of despair over hope, it is possible that the "sleep

of death" might be a never-ending nightmare; the acceptance of despair made permanent. Ay, there indeed is the
rub. It is the dread of something after death, the undiscov-
ered country from whence no traveler returns, that makes
us rather bear those ills we have than fly to others that we
know not of. This, at any rate, is the response of the thought-
ful Christian to thoughts of suicide. It is not, however, the
response of the thoughtless Romeo, who imagines that his
self-slaughter will establish his "everlasting rest" with Juliet:

> I still will stay with thee,
> And never from this palace of dim night
> Depart again. Here, here will I remain
> With worms that are thy chambermaids. O, here
> Will I set up my everlasting rest,
> And shake the yoke of inauspicious stars
> From this world-wearied flesh. Eyes, look your last.
> Arms, take your last embrace. And, lips, O you
> The doors of breath, seal with a righteous kiss
> A dateless bargain to engrossing death!
>
> (5.3.106–15)

Romeo is as thoughtless of the consequences of his actions
in death as he had been of such consequences throughout
his life. As he decides upon self-slaughter and the explicit
rejection of life and its Creator that it signifies, he does not
pause to ponder the possible eternal consequences of such
a choice. He is making his own deathbed and is prepared
to lie in it for eternity. Once again, we are reminded of the
ghostly presence of Paolo and Francesca, the infernal anti-
types of Shakespeare's "star-crossed lovers".

In Romeo's final moments we see the return of the symbolic connection between Romeo's kissing of Juliet and
the poisonous transmission of sin that had characterized

their first kiss only three days earlier. With the deadly poison still on his lips, Romeo's last act is to kiss Juliet: "Thus with a kiss I die" (5.3.120). This last kiss reminds us of the first:

> *Romeo.* Thus from my lips by thine my sin is purg'd.
> *Juliet.* Then have my lips the sin that they have took.
> *Romeo.* Sin from my lips? O trespass sweetly urg'd!
> Give me my sin again.   [*Kissing her.*]
>
> (1.5.105–8)

The metaphor of the "sinful kiss" had caused Juliet to exclaim in alarm that she has succumbed to a sinful act in permitting herself to be kissed by the stranger. As discussed earlier, Shakespeare's use of the "sin" metaphor suggests a clear moral dimension to the exchange. The kiss does not merely transmit the sin metaphorically; it does so literally. Thus the physical poison on Romeo's dying lips as he kisses Juliet for the last time is symbolic of the spiritual poison on his lips when he had first kissed her.

This sin-poison metaphor reminds us of *Hamlet*, in which it plays a crucial role, culminating in its axiomatic place in the play's poisonous and bloody climax. This being so, the parallels between the two plays are worth exploring, not least for their elucidation of Shakespeare's use of this particular metaphor to denote the drama's underpinning moral dynamic.

Whereas in *Romeo and Juliet* the poison of sin is transmitted via the lips of the lovers, in *Hamlet* it is transmitted via the ear of the victim. Claudius murders Hamlet's father by pouring poison into his ear, whereas, later in the play, he poisons Laertes' ear, with equally fatal results, through the poison of his deceitful words. The connection between sin and poison is reinforced when King Claudius fabricates

a story in which he claims that a report of Laertes' prowess
with the rapier had aroused Hamlet's envy:

> Sir, this report of his
> Did Hamlet so envenom with his envy
> That he could nothing do but wish and beg
> Your sudden coming o'er to play with you.
>
> (*Hamlet*, 4.7.102–5)

This juxtaposition of poison and sin, venom and envy, serves
as a fitting prelude to the King's hatching of the scheme
in which he and Laertes will conspire to murder Hamlet
with poison. The King pours the poison of infernal rhet-
oric into Laertes' unknowing ear, killing him with the
venom of his words as surely as the envenomed sword will
kill him later.

Once the symbolic connection between sin and poison
is established, the whole bloody climax of *Hamlet* is seen
in a new anagogical light. The poisoned sword is the cross
upon which Hamlet, the faithful Christian, is crucified.
He is killed not so much by the sword (cross) itself but by
the poison (sin) upon it. In the light of this crucial sin-
poison metaphor, we can see Laertes as the Good Thief of
Scripture, justly killed by the poison (sin) on the sword
(cross), asking for forgiveness and obtaining it before he
dies. From this anagogical perspective it is providential, and
therefore artistically necessary, for Laertes to be killed by
the poison of his own sword, i.e., his own treachery, and
not through the mere *accident* of drinking from the bowl.
Meanwhile, King Claudius emerges as a figure of Satan,
or the satanic, whose treachery becomes apparent at the
moment of climax (the symbolic crucifixion) and who dis-
covers to his horror that he is destroyed by the power of
his own poison. In similar fashion, Romeo is killed by his

own poison, spiritually through his sinful acts and physically through the suicide itself. In both plays, the sin-poison motif provides providential symmetry and moral balance, highlighting the connection between physical actions and metaphysical consequences.

This providential dimension is brought to the fore by the arrival, shortly after Romeo's death, of Friar Lawrence. As Juliet regains consciousness, he urges her to depart from the bloody scene, declaring that "a greater power than we can contradict hath thwarted our intents" (5.3.153–54). This "greater power" is God himself, or his providence, since his is the only power in the cosmos that ultimately cannot be contradicted. The Friar, as an orthodox Christian, cannot be speaking of the devil because Satan has no ultimate power to thwart the intentions of those virtuous souls who seek to contradict his will. Satan can try to seduce the soul, to tempt it, but he cannot force his will upon it. Satan is a seducer because he does not have the power to be a rapist.

The realization that the "greater power" of providence, of God himself, has thwarted the intentions of the lovers, and of Friar Lawrence, raises some difficult but crucial questions. Is it God's will that the lovers should die, or, worse, that they should commit suicide? If it is, does this make God ultimately responsible for their deaths? Is God to blame? The answers to such questions dazzle us with paradox. God does not *will* that the lovers commit suicide, but he does permit them to do so; and yet he is not ultimately to blame. In order to unlock this seemingly bewildering paradox we must understand orthodox theology. The Christian understanding of man is that he is made in God's own image in a way that distinguishes him from the rest of physical creation. One of the key aspects of God's image in man is the gift of free will. God made man free, in the sense that he is not the slave of instinct and in the sense that he can make choices. If freedom means the freedom to choose it must also include the freedom to choose wrongly. If God permitted us to make only the right choices, we would not really be free to choose. Yet God does not *will* us to choose wrongly; on the contrary, he wills us to choose rightly, which is why he has given us the gifts of faith and reason to enable us to make the right choices. But these gifts, though freely given by God, can be freely refused or abused. God does not *will* anyone to make evil choices, and he gives us the means to learn how to make good choices, but his gift of freedom means that we still have the ability to make the evil choices if we insist on doing so. God values the freedom that he has given us so highly that he will never enslave us. We can only enslave ourselves through the choices that we make, which is why we are ultimately to blame for our abuse of the freedom we have been given. In short, and to return to our initial paradoxical questions, God does not will that the lovers should commit suicide, but he gives them the power to do so. He is, however, not to blame because we are ultimately responsible for the choices that we make freely. The overarching paradox is that freedom is not free. It is always married to responsibility. If freedom is divorced from responsibility, self-inflicted disaster ensues. And this is the moral paradox at the heart of *Romeo and Juliet*.

Having made the connection between God's providence and the play's accelerating denouement, Friar Lawrence makes a wrong choice that will have deadly consequences. Overcome with fear at the presence of the dead bodies of Paris and Romeo, and hearing in the distance the imminent arrival of the authorities, he tells Juliet that he "dare no longer stay" (5.3.159) and urges her to leave the scene of carnage and "contagion" (5.3.152). Juliet refuses to leave, and the Friar flees from her presence, abandoning her in his cowardice to the extremes of passion that would lead to her own suicide.

As Juliet approaches her own self-slaughter, Shakespeare resurrects the sin-kiss-poison metaphor, thereby once again dexterously connecting the lovers' first sinful kiss with their poisonous last embrace: "I will kiss thy lips; / Haply some poison yet doth hang on them, / To make me die with a restorative" (5.3.164–66). After kissing his still warm lips, Juliet takes Romeo's dagger and fatally stabs herself with it: "O, happy dagger! / This is thy sheath; there rust, and let me die" (5.3.168–69). The sexual imagery, in which Romeo's dagger takes on phallic significance as it invaginates itself in Juliet's willingly receptive body, is pregnant with the symbolic symmetry with which Shakespeare informs his work. In this case, paradoxically, the pregnancy of the symbolism is wedded to the sterility of the symbol. The symbolism of Juliet's final coital embrace with Romeo's dagger points to the barrenness and deadliness of the sexual union when it is divorced from the virtues and responsibilities commensurate with marriage and parenthood.

After the watchmen discover the carnage in the sepulchre, including the body of Juliet, "bleeding, warm, and newly dead" (5.3.174), they hasten to summon the Prince to the scene of desolation, along with the Capulets and the Montagues. "O wife, look how our daughter bleeds!" Capulet exclaims, adding that Romeo's dagger had "mis-sheathed in my daughter's bosom" (5.3.201, 204). Lady Capulet's response serves as a clarion call, a *carillon* that invites us to employ our moral imagination to make sense of the carnage and the carrion that we see before us:

O me! this sight of death is as a bell
That warns my old age to a sepulchre.

(5.3.205–6)

Although these words are often taken as meaning that Lady
Capulet now wishes that she too were dead, her life not
being worth living after the death of her daughter, we should
not forget their employment in this context as a memento
mori, a literary device or motif that was very popular in
mediaeval art and literature and which was employed widely
by Shakespeare in his own works, signifying his own profound orthodoxy. The moral purpose of the memento mori
is to remind us of death, judgment, heaven, and hell, the
four last things of Christian theology that Romeo and Juliet
had so brazenly forgotten or defied. The death of the lovers serves as a warning bell, reminding Lady Capulet, and
Shakespeare's audience, of the mortality of the body and
the immortality of the soul. Thus Lady Capulet's words serve
to reorient the audience toward the moral vision that the
play's denouement will reflect. The warning bell is nothing
less than a wake-up call.

Now that Shakespeare has our full attention, the moral
that he sets before us is iterated and reiterated in the lines
that follow. "Meantime forbear," commands the Prince, "and
let mischance be slave to patience" (5.3.219–20). Although
these lines are usually passed over as nothing but a call for
calm, they are literally a demand for the restoration of a
true moral vision. Henceforth, misadventure must be obe-
dient to the dictates of patience and must not be left to run
amok in an impatient, intemperate, and imprudent frenzy,
as has been the case up to this point. Mischance must be
made a slave to patience because, if it is not, if, on the
contrary, patience is made a slave to mischance, a reign of

ruinous anarchy will prevail. Indeed, as no doubt we are
meant to acknowledge, such anarchy has already reigned ruin-
ously in the lives of the two suicidal lovers. Enough of such
nonsense, the Prince seems to be saying, it is time to rectify
this disastrous reversal of the true moral order. Henceforth,
patience and not mischance must hold sway. And let's not
forget the gravity of the verb phrase "to forbear", particularly with regard to its connection with the triumph of patience
over "mischance". "To forbear" is to abstain or refrain from
an action in deference to moral imperatives. Throughout
the play, Romeo and Juliet have consistently refused to forbear, indulging their passions in pursuit of the instant gratification of momentary desire. Indeed, the only thing that
the lovers consistently forbore was forbearance itself! Such
madness must stop, the Prince commands. His subjects must
forbear, thereby tempering mischance with patience.

The Prince's wisdom is reiterated by Friar Lawrence in
the midst of his candid confession of the role he played in
the unraveling of the tragedy. Upon Juliet's awakening, he
had "entreated" her to come forth from the tomb and "bear
this work of heaven with patience" (5.3.259–60). Since God,
in his providence, had permitted the systematic denial and
defiance of virtue to lead to such a deadly debauch of self-
inflicted suffering, Juliet should learn her lesson. She must
forbear, making mischance the slave of patience. Instead,
she chooses to follow the passionate desire of the moment
to its fatal conclusion, making patience the slave of mischance. In refusing to "bear this work of heaven" she is
perhaps freely choosing her hell. Bearing in mind her age,
and her upbringing, we might hope that, in spite of herself, she will receive God's mercy and not his justice. One
wonders, however, if even the mercy of God can save a
soul that pointedly refuses to desire heaven.

Should Shakespeare's audience have failed to get the message or understand the moral in the Prince's command and the Friar's "entreaty", it is spelled out again, in no uncertain terms, in the unequivocal way in which the Prince connects punishment to Providence:

> ... Capulet, Montague,
> See what a scourge is laid upon your hate,
> That heaven finds means to kill your joys with love!
> And I, for winking at your discords too,
> Have lost a brace of kinsmen. All are punish'd.
>
> (5.3.290–94)

Providence has outwitted and outmaneuvered the hatred of the families and the disordered eros of the lovers, punishing the sinners for their transgressions. Thus the play's denouement is not a meaningless mess, as many modern critics would have us believe, but a revelation of God's hand at work in the cosmos. The question is not, therefore, one relating to God's absence from the play, since he is quite clearly present; it is rather a question relating to the sort of God who *is* present. Is he truly a loving God, or is he simply a killjoy, scourging not only the hatred of the Montagues and Capulets but the love of Romeo and Juliet? Is he in fact perverse, choosing to kill the joys of those who hate by literally killing those who love? Does he punish those who believe in an eye for an eye by kissing them Judas-like on the very cheek that they refuse to turn, betraying their loved ones to their deaths? The answer is to be found in the double entendre implicit in the way in which God scourges *"with love"*: "heaven finds means to kill your joys with love". This line is often read with its ironic meaning in mind without paying due attention to the deep theology present in the double entendre. It is indeed ironic that the hatred is scourged with the love that Romeo and Juliet had for each other. If they had not fallen in love, they would not have become what Capulet calls the "poor sacrifices of our enmity".[1] This is true and it is ironic. Yet the deeper irony is present in the deeper truth to be found in the double entendre. The most profound truth is that God's punishment is always given "with love". God *is* love; he hates nobody, not even the most miserable sinner. He shows this love most powerfully in the way in which he was himself scourged and put to death for the sins of others. He was scourged so that he could redeem those who hate like Montague and Capulet and love like Romeo and Juliet. In this sense, the whole of *Romeo and Juliet* is a re-presentation in microcosm of the mystery of redemption. Although suffering is present because of sin, God brings reconciliation, finding means to scourge the families "with love" so that, through suffering, they are finally able to see the truth. As such, the scourging is actually the curing of the sin, the means by which the families' hatred is turned to reconciliatory love. This had been prophesied in the opening lines of the play, in which the Chorus had proclaimed of Romeo and Juliet that "their death" will "bury their parents' strife" which "but their children's end . . . nought could remove" (1. prol. 8–11). From its beginning to its end,

---

[1] 5.3.303. Literally, the "poor sacrifices" are the gold statues that the two families erect as a mark of their reconciliation. Of these statues, Andrew J. Harvey writes: "Shakespeare asks us not to see their golden statues as idols inspired by bad theology or as graven images of impetuous love but as 'sacrifices of [their families'] enmity', as symbols of forgiveness, and as the affirmation of that 'pity sitting in the clouds / That sees into the bottom of . . . grief' (5.3.303; 3.5.197–98)" (Andrew J. Harvey, "The Crossing of Love: Shakespeare's Chiastic Wit in *Romeo and Juliet*", in William Shakespeare, *Romeo and Juliet*, ed. Joseph Pearce, Ignatius Critical Editions [San Francisco: Ignatius Press, 2011], p. 204).

therefore, *Romeo and Juliet* is nothing less than an affirmation of that "pity sitting in the clouds that sees into the bottom of grief" (3.5.197). It is, therefore, singularly appropriate that the Prince's final words, and the final lines of the play, should constitute another climactic memento mori, reminding us yet again of the four last things:

> A glooming peace this morning with it brings;
> The sun for sorrow will not show his head.
> Go hence, to have more talk of these sad things;
> Some shall be pardon'd, and some punished;
> For never was a story of more woe
> Than this of Juliet and her Romeo.

(5.3.304–9)

We will all die; we will all be judged; some will be pardoned; some will be punished. This is the Prince's final piece of wisdom for the assembled people of Verona; this is Shakespeare's final piece of wisdom for us, his audience. Nor is it wisdom that should be taken lightly or forgotten, but, on the contrary, and as the Prince emphasizes, it is wisdom to be heeded and taught to everyone we meet: "Go hence, to have more talk of these sad things."

EPILOGUE: DOES *ROMEO AND JULIET* HAVE A HAPPY ENDING?

Throughout the play, the palpable absence of the cardinal virtues of prudence and temperance paves the way for the denouement of the tragedy. The absence of such virtue in the lovers is exacerbated by its absence in other crucial characters who, being older, are perhaps even more culpable than the play's principal protagonists. Friar Lawrence begins by giving sagacious advice but fails to practice what he preaches in his rash agreement to marry the lovers in undue haste; Capulet begins with a seeming desire to protect his child from a premature marriage but then insists upon forcing her into an unwanted marriage to Paris; the Nurse fails to support Juliet, even suggesting that her young charge proceed with the bigamous marriage. It is clear, therefore, that Juliet is betrayed by those who should have saved her from her own immature folly. This failure on the part of the adult characters serves as a moral counterpoint to the treacherous passions of youth. It is as though Shakespeare is illustrating that the young will go tragically astray if not restrained by the wisdom, virtue, and example of their elders. The final tragedy is that this lesson is only learned by the Capulets and Montagues in the wake of the deaths of their children. The lesson *is* learned, however, and the consequent restoration of peace provides a sad but consoling catharsis. Whether such a cathartic turn can be considered a happy ending is a moot point. It is, however, an ending that restores not only peace but sanity to the surviving protagonists, and this is surely a source of joy, even if a joy tinted with sorrow.

Ultimately the peace that reigns at the end of *Romeo and Juliet* is much greater than the worldly and merely political peace that emerges in Verona. It is the peace that "passes all understanding", as Saint Paul tells the Philippians (Phil 4:7), the peace that T. S. Eliot proclaims at the culmination and climax of *The Waste Land*, and the peace that descends on the so-called tragic climaxes of *Hamlet* and *King Lear*. It is the knowledge imparted in the midst of the tragedy by Friar Lawrence that "a greater power than we can contradict hath thwarted our intents" (5.3.153–54). The greater power of divine providence is not contradicted. Its harmony and its peace remain. It cannot be thwarted by the imprudent impudence of our sinful intentions and actions. God's will is done at the end of *Romeo and Juliet* as it is done at the end of *Hamlet* and *Lear*. It is a will that dictates that all will suffer as a consequence of sin, even the apparently blameless, but that the virtuous and the penitent will receive mercy, whereas the wicked will reap the bitter harvest of their sins, the just deserts for their unjust actions. Such peace is not of the sort that the world understands or desires. It is a peace that can only be perceived through the eyes of faith, a faith the world does not know and cannot offer, a faith that finds voice in the greatest art and finds the divine comedy in the midst of the greatest tragedies.

APPENDIX: THE JESUIT CONNECTION

The Jesuit poet and martyr Saint Robert Southwell was executed in London on February 20, 1595, shortly before Shakespeare is thought to have begun work on *Romeo and Juliet*. Since there is abundant evidence to suggest that Shakespeare knew Southwell and that he admired Southwell's poetry, and since Southwell's influence on *The Merchant of Venice*, a play that was written at around the same time as *Romeo and Juliet*, has been documented convincingly, it is worth examining the evidence for Southwell's influence on Shakespeare's characterization of the "star-crossed lovers". First, however, let's summarize the biographical and textual evidence for Shakespeare's acquaintance with Southwell.[1]

Although Shakespeare and Southwell were distant cousins it is likely that they first met through their mutual relationship with the young Earl of Southampton, Henry Wriothesley, who was Shakespeare's patron. Since the evidence shows that Southwell was probably Southampton's confessor and spiritual adviser at the time that Shakespeare and Southampton first met, it brings Shakespeare into the orbit of the most famous and feared Jesuit in England. Indeed, since Shakespeare, Southampton, and Southwell were all denizens of London's Catholic recusant underground it seems

[1] A more extensive discussion of this evidence is given in Joseph Pearce, *The Quest for Shakespeare: The Bard of Avon and the Church of Rome* (San Francisco: Ignatius Press, 2008), and also in Joseph Pearce, *Through Shakespeare's Eyes: Seeing the Catholic Presence in the Plays* (San Francisco: Ignatius Press, 2010).

very likely that each would have been on intimate terms with the other.

Apart from their mutual acquaintance with the Earl of Southampton, and the strong circumstantial evidence that they must have known each other within the confines of the close-knit recusant community, the strongest evidence for Southwell's and Shakespeare's friendship is to be found in their respective works. Southwell's writing, in poetry and prose, was very widely read, even by his sworn enemies, such as Lord Burghley, Francis Bacon, Richard Topcliffe, and even the Queen herself. As for his friends in the persecuted Catholic community, his works were devoured avidly. He was not merely a priest who had somehow eluded capture since his arrival in England in 1586 but was a true poet whose place in the literary canon, centuries later, is assured. Is it any wonder, therefore, that Shakespeare, as a Catholic and as a poet, should be drawn to this particular Jesuit?

Shortly before his capture in July 1592, Southwell had been working on a manuscript of his poems and had penned three separate dedications for different sections of his work, the first being a preface addressed to the author's "Loving Cousin". Since Southwell and Shakespeare were distant cousins it has been conjectured that the preface was addressed to Shakespeare, though others have suggested that the "Cousin" in question was perhaps Southampton, since Southwell's brother and sister had each married Southampton's first cousins. Either way, the preface itself is an appeal to poets in general, or perhaps to Shakespeare in particular, to use their God-given talents in the service of the Giver of them:

> Poets, by abusing their talents, and making the follies and feignings of love the customary subject of their base endeavours, have so discredited this faculty, that a poet, a lover,

and a liar, are by many reckoned but three words of one signification ... [T]he Devil ... hath ... possessed ... most poets with his idle fancies. For in lieu of solemn and devout matters, to which in duty they owe their abilities, [poets] now busy themselves in expressing such passions as serve only for testimonies to what unworthy affections they have wedded their wills. And because the best course to let them see the error of their works is to weave a new web in their own loom, I have here laid a few coarse threads together to invite some skillfuller wits to go forward in the same, or to begin some finer piece, wherein may be seen how well verse and virtue suit together. Blame me not (good Cousin) though I send you a blameworthy present, in which the most that can commend it, is the good will of the writer.[2]

Such an exhortation to poets to wed their verse to virtue, coming as it does from a Jesuit priest, may be of little surprise perhaps and may seem to have little direct relevance to Shakespeare per se as distinct from poets in general. But if this preface is taken in conjunction with another dedication by Southwell, this time addressed from "The Author to the Reader", a picture begins to emerge that perhaps the Jesuit had Shakespeare specifically in mind:

Still finest wits are 'stilling Venus' rose.
In paynim toys the sweetest veins are spent:
To Christian works, few have their talents lent ...

You heavenly sparks of wit shew native light,
Cloud not with misty loves your orient clear ...

[2] Robert Southwell, S.J., *The Poems of Robert Southwell, S.J.* James H. McDonald and Nancy Pollard Brown, eds. (London: Oxford University Press, 1967), pp. 1–2. The spelling has been modernized for purposes of clarification.

Favour my wish, well-wishing works no ill;
I move the suit the grant rests in your will.[3]

Again, there is nothing at first sight that makes this new exhortation specific to Shakespeare. From the late Renaissance onward, poets and artists had looked to Pagan antiquity as the fire for their Muse and had increasingly turned their backs on the Christocentric Muse of their mediaeval forebears. Why should we conclude that such a complaint about the "finest wits" wasting their powers on "paynim toys" has anything to do with Shakespeare in particular? The clue is to be found in the first and last lines of Southwell's verse, as quoted. The line about the "finest wits" distilling "Venus' rose" has been seen as a reference to Shakespeare's poem *Venus and Adonis*, especially when coupled with the assumption of a pun on Shakespeare's name in the last line: "I move the suit, the grant rests in your *will*." In other words, Southwell has made the request that the "finest wit" of the poet should be employed on something worthier than the pagan toys of Venus, but that the granting of the request rests with "Will". The fact that Southwell's "suit", in the final line, is said to rest in "*your* will" has caused some observers to surmise that this dedication is not addressed to Shakespeare directly but to Southampton as Shakespeare's patron.

If this evidence raises eyebrows but still fails to convince the skeptical reader of the connection between Southwell and Shakespeare, the third dedication by Southwell addressed "to my worthy good cousin, Master W. S." should prove decisive. Should the skeptic point out that Southwell must have known others with the same initials as Shakespeare,

<hr />

[3] Ibid., p. 75.

notwithstanding the significance of his being a "cousin", the connection with "poets" and the apparent punning reference to "Will", there is yet more evidence that surely puts the Shakespearean connection beyond doubt. When Southwell's poems were published shortly after he was brutally executed as a "traitor" in 1595, the dedication was shortened so that it was addressed merely "to my worthy good cousin". The reason for the omission of the name is obvious enough. Southwell was a pariah in the eyes of the state, vilified for his "treason", and "Master W. S." would no doubt have been similarly vilified should his identity become known. It is, therefore, significant that the name does not finally appear in an edition of Southwell's poems until an edition published in 1616, the year of Shakespeare's death! It was only then that "Master W. S.", the martyred Jesuit's "worthy good cousin", was finally beyond the reach of possible persecution.

There is further corroborating evidence of the connection between Shakespeare and Southwell in the dedicatory letter that Shakespeare wrote to Southampton for *Venus and Adonis.*

To the Right Honorable Henry Wriothesley,
Earl of Southampton, and Baron of Titchfield.

Right Honorable,

I know not how I shall offend in dedicating my unpolished lines to your Lordship, nor how the world will censure me for choosing so strong a prop to support so weak a burden, only if your Honor seem but pleased, I account myself highly praised, and vow to take advantage of all idle hours, till I have honored you with some graver labor. But if the first heir of my invention prove deformed, I shall be sorry it had so noble a godfather: and never after ear [i.e.,

plough] so barren a land, for fear it yield me still so bad a
harvest, I leave it to your Honorable survey, and your Honor
to your heart's content which I wish may always answer
your own wish, and the world's hopeful expectation.

Your Honor's in all duty,
William Shakespeare.

The key here, perhaps, lies in the apology for the nature of
the poem and a promise to produce "some graver labor".
This, of course, is exactly what Robert Southwell had urged
that he do. It could perhaps be argued that the words should
not be taken in this way and that, in fact, they are merely
words of self-deprecation as befits a dedicatory letter to one's
patron. Perhaps this is so. And yet the timing of these various
works is persuasive in support of the former possibility. Southwell was working on his poems, and had written the various
dedications, shortly before his arrest in July 1592. Shakespeare's poem was registered for printing on April 18, 1593,
but surely it is likely that a poem of almost twelve hundred
lines would have been many months in the making, especially if we assume, as we must, that Shakespeare had rela-
tively few "idle hours" for poetry in the midst of his other
commitments, not least of which was the writing of *Richard III*. Southwell may have heard from Southampton, or from
Shakespeare himself, that Shakespeare had *begun* work on an
epic poem on the subject of Venus and Adonis, prompting
his complaint in the second dedication about the "finest wits"
distilling the goddess' rose and playing with pagan toys, instead
of employing their talents on more serious or "graver" Christian work. If this were so, the promise that "some graver labor"
would follow must be seen as a nod of recognition between
the poet and his patron in the direction of their friend, now
imprisoned and destined, no doubt, for martyrdom.

The connection is strengthened further by the fact that Shakespeare's next work, on which he was working, presumably, throughout 1593 and the early part of 1594, when Southwell was still languishing in prison, was *The Rape of Lucrece*. According to the historian and literary critic Hugh Ross Williamson, "the atmosphere of *Lucrece* is so very different from that of *Venus and Adonis* that it is not impossible to suppose, even were there no other evidence, that Southampton had rightly read Southwell's dedication: 'I move the suit; the grant rests in your Will', and that Shakespeare, moved by Southwell's dedication to him, had tried to use his talent to a worthier end and, under the form of a 'fable', had written of the violation of a soul by sin."[4] In doing so, Shakespeare may have had Southwell's own words about the power of "fables" in mind. In the preface to his *Mary Magdalen's Funeral Tears*, published in 1591, Southwell had written: "In fables are often figured moral truths and that covertly uttered to a common good which, without mask, would not find so free a passage." Although it is almost certain that Shakespeare had read this poem by Southwell, together with its preface, it is possible also that the two men had discussed the means of conveying "moral truths . . . covertly", through the power of art, during their friendship prior to the priest's arrest. In any event, many critics have highlighted the similarities between Southwell's poetry and Shakespeare's. John W. Hales, in his preface to T. H. Ward's *English Poets*, comments on how curiously reminiscent Shakespeare's *Rape of Lucrece* is to Southwell's *St. Peter's Complaint*, and Christopher Devlin, in his life of Southwell, expends several pages comparing

[4] Hugh Ross Williamson, *The Day Shakespeare Died* (London: Michael Joseph, 1962), p. 58.

parallel passages from each of the works to highlight the similarities. He concludes with the opinion that Shakespeare's poem had been influenced directly by Southwell's: "[T]he general impression one gets—quite independently of any external evidence—is that Shakespeare, pricked by Southwell's example, had tried his hand at tapping a loftier and more metaphysical vein." [5]

There is a curious postscript to this whole discussion of Southwell's influence on Shakespeare's early poetry. If a recent reading of the poem is to be believed, Southwell's judgment of Shakespeare's motives for writing *Venus and Adonis* was a little premature, especially if he ascribed only neopagan, or more correctly merely pseudo-pagan, motives for distilling the flower of the goddess into verse. Richard Wilson, in "A Bloody Question: The Politics of *Venus and Adonis*",[6] has argued that the iconography of *Venus and Adonis* suggests that the poem is a critique of the martyr's cause pursued by Southwell and also of the persecution of Catholics brought on by Queen Elizabeth. In its elaborate phraseology, Wilson argues, Elizabeth emerges as the predatory tyrannical Venus and Lord Burghley as the boar who kills Adonis. If this reading is correct, Shakespeare presumably transformed his Venus poem, which was probably written, for the most part, after Southwell's arrest, into the "graver labor" that Southwell had himself requested. It is, in fact, Shakespeare's tribute to Southwell. Such a conclusion is supported by the Latin epigraph that Shakespeare chose for the poem:

---

[5] Christopher Devlin, *The Life of Robert Southwell* (New York: Farrar, Straus and Cudahy, 1956), p. 273.

[6] Richard Wilson, "A Bloody Question: The Politics of *Venus and Adonis'*, *Religion and the Arts* 5, no. 3 (2001): 297–316.

Vilia miretur vulgus: mihi flavus Apollo
Pocula Castalia plena ministret aqua.

Taken from a poem by Ovid, the lines may be translated thus:

Let base conceited wits admire vile things,
Fair Phoebus lead me to the muses' springs.[7]

The choice of such an epigraph can be seen as Shakespeare's own positive response to Southwell's complaint that poets, "by abusing their talents", have made "the follies and feignings of love" the subject of "their base endeavours", so that "the devil . . . hath possessed . . . most poets with his idle fancies" so that "in lieu of solemn and devout matters, to which in duty they owe their abilities, they now busy themselves in expressing such passions as serve only for testimonies to what unworthy affections they have wedded their wills". Instead of succumbing to these lower passions, Southwell had urged his "loving cousin" (presumably Shakespeare) "to begin some finer piece, wherein may be seen how well verse and virtue suit together". In responding to Southwell's challenge, Shakespeare seems to have especially chosen an epigraph for his poem to serve as a personal reply to the imprisoned Jesuit and as an endorsement of his plaintive words.

During the time that Shakespeare was presumably writing *Venus and Adonis*, in the latter half of 1592, Southwell was imprisoned at the home of Elizabeth's chief torturer, Richard Topcliffe. He was repeatedly tortured in the vain hope that he could be made to betray other priests. His astounding courage in the midst of such excruciating suffering extracted a grudging tribute even from one of his sworn

---

[7] Christopher Marlowe's translation of Ovid's lines quoted in Francis Cunningham, ed., *The Works of Christopher Marlowe including his Translations* (London: Chatto & Windus, 1902), p. 238.

enemies, Robert Cecil, Lord Burghley's son, who, having
witnessed Southwell being tortured, admitted to a friend:
"They boast about the heroes of antiquity ... but we have a
new torture which it is not possible for a man to bear. And
yet I have seen Robert Southwell hanging by it, still as a tree
trunk, and no one able to drag one word from his mouth." [8]

Southwell was moved from Topcliffe's house to the Gate-
house in Westminster and thence to the Tower of London,
where he was tortured on a further ten occasions. On February 20, 1595, almost three years after his arrest and imprisonment, he was hanged, drawn, and quartered at Tyburn in
London. Standing in the cart, beneath the gibbet and with
the noose around his neck, he made the sign of the cross
and recited a passage from Romans, chapter fourteen.[9] When
the sheriff tried to interrupt him, those in the crowd, many
of whom were sympathetic to the Jesuit's plight, shouted
that he should be allowed to speak. He confessed that he
was a Jesuit priest and prayed for the salvation of the Queen
and his country. As the cart was drawn away he commended
his soul to God in the same words that Christ had used from
the Cross: *In manus tuas* ... (Into your hands, Lord, I commend my spirit [see Lk 23:46]). As he hung in the noose,
some onlookers pushed forward and tugged at his legs to
hasten his death before he could be cut down and disembow-
eled alive. Southwell was thirty-three years old, the same
age as Christ at the time of his Crucifixion.

Was Shakespeare at this grisly scene? Did he add his voice
to those doing their best to comfort the doomed Jesuit?
We will never know the answers to such questions. We do

---

[8] Williamson, *Day Shakespeare Died*, p. 57.

[9] "If we live, we live to the Lord, and if we die, we die to the Lord; so
then, whether we live or whether we die, we are the Lord's" (Rom 14:8).

know, however, that there is ample evidence to suggest that Shakespeare knew Robert Southwell, and perhaps that he knew him well. It seems also that the martyred Jesuit had inspired some of Shakespeare's finest poetry.

If *Venus and Adonis* is, as Richard Wilson suggests, a cryptic fable in which Venus (Elizabeth) is a predator, and Burghley is the boar that kills Adonis (Southwell), we can see that Shakespeare did as Southwell had asked. He had composed a fable in which moral truths are figured covertly. In the years ahead Southwell's "cousin" would continue to use his art to convey truths, "covertly uttered to a common good which, without mask, would not find so free a passage".

With regard to Southwell's continuing influence on Shakespeare, we might expect to see his ghostly presence most in evidence in the works that Shakespeare was writing in the wake of the Jesuit's brutal execution. It is, therefore, not surprising to see covert references to Southwell and his work in both *Romeo and Juliet* and *The Merchant of Venice*, both of which were written at this time.

Shakespeare would have been writing *The Merchant of Venice* shortly after Southwell's execution or, if we accept the earliest possible dates for the play's composition, during the period in which the Jesuit was being tortured repeatedly by Richard Topcliffe, Elizabeth's sadistic chief interrogator. It should not surprise us, therefore, that we see Southwell's shadow, or shade, in Shakespeare's play. It is present most palpably in the haunting echoes of Southwell's own poetry, which Shakespeare evidently knew well and which he introduces into *The Merchant of Venice* on numerous occasions.[10]

---

[10] I am indebted in this discussion of Saint Robert Southwell's influence on *The Merchant of Venice* to the diligent research of John Klause. See John Klause, "Catholic and Protestant, Jesuit and Jew: Historical Religion in *The*

Take, for instance, Portia's words after the Prince of Aragon's failure in the test of the caskets: "Thus hath the candle sing'd the moth" (2.9.79). And compare it to lines from Southwell's "Lewd Love Is Losse":

> So long the flie doth dallie with the flame,
> Untill his singed wings doe force his fall.[11]

Not only does the phraseology suggest Shakespeare's indebtedness to Southwell, but the very title of the poem from which the phrase is extracted suggests a connection to Shakespeare's theme that lewd love is loss. Aragon's love is lewdly self-interested, and his choice leads to the loss of his hopes to marry Portia. Shakespeare is not simply taking lines from Southwell; he is apparently taking his very theme from him, a theme that would be even more to the fore in *Romeo and Juliet*.

In the final act of *The Merchant of Venice*, as Portia and Nerissa return to Belmont, they see a candle burning in the darkness. "When the moon shone, we did not see the candle", says Nerissa, to which the sagacious Portia responds: "So doth the greater glory dim the less" (5.1.92–93). Compare this to Southwell's "seeking the sunne it is . . . booteles to borrowe the light of a candle".[12] The greater glory dims the less, so sing Southwell and Shakespeare in harmony. The candle is dimmed by the light of the moon, and the moon is dimmed by the light of the sun, and the sun is dimmed by the Light of the World himself, the One Source from

---

Merchant of Venice", in Dennis Taylor and David N. Beauregard, eds., *Shakespeare and the Culture of Christianity in Early Modern England* (New York: Fordham University Press, 2003), pp. 180–221.

[11] Southwell, "Lewd Love Is Losse" in *Poems of Robert Southwell*, pp. 62–63.

[12] Robert Southwell, *Marie Magdalens Funeral Teares*, ed. Vincent B. Leitch (Delmar, N.Y.: Scholars' Facsimiles and Reprints, 1974); quoted in Taylor and Beauregard, *Shakespeare and the Culture of Christianity*, p. 187.

whom the celestial firmament receives its light. Once again, Southwell's theme is Shakespeare's, the latter seemingly paying homage to the former.

It is also intriguing that an expression ascribed by the *Oxford English Dictionary* to Shakespeare's coinage was actually coined originally by Southwell, to whom Shakespeare was presumably indebted. The phrase is Shylock's "a wilderness of monkeys" (subsequent to "a wilderness of Tygers" in *Titus Andronicus*), which owed its original source to Southwell's "a wilderness of serpents" in his *Epistle unto his Father*.[13]

If the foregoing should fail to convince the skeptical reader of Southwell's ghostly presence, the pivotal scene in which Bassanio triumphs in the wisdom of his choice to "hazard all he hath", i.e., lay down his life for his love, should prove sufficient to allay the most hardened skepticism. The Shakespeare scholar John Klause has shown how this scene resonates as an echo of Southwell's *Marie Magdalens Funeral Teares*, in which the saint is of a mind to "venture [her] life" for her love of her Lord. Klause shows many suggestive parallels between Shakespeare's scene and Southwell's earlier work, and yet nowhere is the allusion to Southwell more evident than in the exchange between Bassanio and Portia before Bassanio makes his choice:

> *Bassanio:*   Let me choose,
>   For as I am, I live upon the rack.
> *Portia:* Upon the rack, Bassanio! then confess
>   What treason there is mingled with your love.
> *Bassanio:* None but that ugly treason of mistrust,
>   Which makes me fear th' enjoying of my love;

[13] Klause, "Religion in *Merchant of Venice*", p. 187. Southwell's *Epistle unto his Father* was written in 1588 or 1589, five years or so before Shakespeare used the similar phrase in *Titus Andronicus*.

There may as well be amity and life
'Tween snow and fire, as treason and my love.
Portia: Ay, but I fear you speak upon the rack,
Where men enforced do speak any thing.
Bassanio: Promise me life, and I'll confess the truth.
Portia: Well then, confess and live.
Bassanio: Confess and love
Had been the very sum of my confession.
O happy torment, when my torturer
Doth teach me answers for deliverance!
But let me to my fortune and the caskets.
Portia: Away then! I am lock'd in one of them;
If you do love me, you will find me out.
                    (*Merchant of Venice* 3.2.24–41)

Since this exchange between the lover and the longed-for beloved comes in the midst of an array of references to Southwell's earlier work, it is difficult to avoid the conclusion that it represents a clear allusion to Southwell's own recent experience "upon the rack" at the hands of a torturer seeking to force him into a confession of the alleged crime of "treason" with which he had been charged. Such a conclusion is reinforced still further when juxtaposed with Southwell's own words in his *Humble Supplication to Her Maiestie*:

> What unsufferable Agonies we have bene put to upon the Rack . . . [One so tortured] is apt to utter anything to abridge the sharpnes and severity of paine. [Yet even an] unskillful Lay man . . . [would] rather venture his life by saying too much, then hazard his Conscience in not answering sufficient.[14]

What else is Bassanio doing, as he ponders the choices presented to him by the caskets, if not venturing his very life in

---

[14] Robert Southwell, *An Humble Supplication to Her Maiestie*, ed. R. C. Bald (Cambridge: Cambridge University Press, 1953), pp. 34–35.

the choice of death (lead) over worldly temptations (gold and silver)? He is willing to "hazard all he hath", as the casket demands, if it is the only way to gain his love. The parallels with Robert Southwell's willingness to die for his faith, hazarding all he has in his willingness to lay down his life for his friends, is obvious. And it is made even more so by the way in which Shakespeare artfully intersperses phrases from yet another of Southwell's works, *St. Peter's Complaint*, into the words that Portia sings as Bassanio prepares to make his choice.[15]

Antonio's willingness to "be racked even to the uttermost" to furnish the means by which Bassanio can win his "fair Portia" is destined to be put to the uttermost test as the drama unfolds. The word "racked" is a portentous pun on "recked" or "reck'd", in the sense of a reckoning, an account that must be paid, or a day of reckoning on which something must be atoned for or avenged, thereby linking the word with the Day of Atonement, the most solemn fast of the Jewish year, and by extension with the Christian Day of Atonement, Good Friday, on which the reconciliation of God and man is achieved through Christ's Crucifixion. The pun is indeed brilliant but should not detract from the literal meaning of the word "racked", i.e., tortured on the rack, which connects the text with the fate of the subtextually omnipresent Southwell. In this way the words "racked" and "recked" become interchangeable. The Merchant and the Jesuit on the rack are mystically united with Christ on the Cross.[16] The racking is the reckoning, the atonement for

---

[15] For details of the similarities between Portia's song and *St. Peter's Complaint*, see Klause, "Religion in *Merchant of Venice*", p. 196.

[16] And the same is true of Shakespeare's use of the imagery of the "rack" as Bassanio prepares for the trial of the caskets. In this case it is Bassanio and Southwell who are mystically united with the crucified Christ as they choose to "hazard all" for their love.

sin. For Antonio, it is not his wealth, or the money that he owes, that will be reckoned and racked. It will be his love for Bassanio, symbolized by the pound of flesh nearest his heart.

We have already discussed the likelihood that Portia's reference to the candle singeing the moth was taken from Robert Southwell's poem "Lewd Love Is Losse":

> So long the flie doth dallie with the flame,
> Untill his singed wings doe force his fall.[17]

The connection between Portia's words and Southwell's poem are further strengthened by Nerissa's words immediately after Portia's allusive words are uttered:

> The ancient saying is no heresy,
> Hanging and wiving goes with destiny.
> (2.9.81–82)

From a Catholic perspective, Robert Southwell was hanged as a priest, and, as a priest, *in persona Christi*, he had chosen the Church as his Bride (hence the vow of celibacy taken by the Catholic clergy). In choosing the Church as his "wife" he had accepted "hanging" as his destiny. Southwell, like all the Jesuit missionaries to Elizabethan England, expected to be brutally put to death if caught by the authorities. Nerissa's words, coming immediately after Portia's allusion to Southwell's poem, can be seen as a coded tribute to the recently martyred or soon to be martyred priest, a fact that is highlighted still further by Nerissa's declaration that the "ancient" is "no heresy", i.e., the old faith was not heretical.

---

[17] Southwell, "Lewd Love Is Losse", in *Poems of Robert Southwell*, p. 91.

Southwell's theme, "Lewd Love Is Losse", is also Shake-speare's. The lewdness of Aragon's love and his dallying with the flames of his own prideful passion have led to the loss of his heart's desire. Portia also perceives with her usual unerring moral perspective that the deliberations of Morocco and Aragon were ultimately foolish because their fallacious philosophies, fueled with pride, have "outwitted" wisdom. Or, to put the matter the other way round, the wisdom of Portia's father had outwitted the "wit" of the worldly-wise. Portia's father knew, as does Portia, that the right to choose is not enough to merit the reward. To win our hearts' desire we must use the right to choose to choose the right.

In order to understand Shakespeare's deepest meaning, we need to learn, with Bassanio, the importance of his choosing the right casket and the logical and theological reasoning by which he does so. We must begin, as Shakespeare does, by reminding ourselves once again of the allusive connection between Bassanio and Robert Southwell. Having heralded Bassanio's arrival, at the end of act 2, with an allusion to the Jesuit's poem, followed by the equally poignant ecclesiological metaphor of the Bride and the Bridegroom, and with the suggestive connection between "hanging and wiving", Bassanio's casket scene continues this allusive theme with Jesuitical dexterity. Portia complains that "these naughty times [put] bars between the owners and their rights", a phrase that suggests a connection between the wicked times in which Shakespeare and his audience found themselves and the imprisonment of those who sought the right to practice their faith without harassment or persecution. For Shakespeare and his Catholic contemporaries, there was no right in law to choose the right. The state's anti-Catholic laws put bars between the Catholic laity and the practice of their faith, and, in the case of priests such as Southwell, put prison bars between them and the faithful they sought to serve. Taken by itself, in isolation from what comes before and after it, the allusion might be considered somewhat tenuous, but taken together with the allusions that precede it and the exchange between Bassanio and Portia about living "upon the rack" which immediately succeeds it, the convergence of so many similar allusive images becomes convincing. Let's assume, therefore, as we look at the unfolding drama of this crucial part of the play, that Shakespeare always has one eye on the ghostly presence of Robert Southwell as he puts his weighty and weighted words into the mouths of his protagonists.

Having perceived the Bard's deeper meaning we are not surprised to discover that Portia's words, as Bassanio prepares to make his choice, are pregnant with theological symbolism.

> He may win,
> And what is music then? Then music is
> Even as the flourish when true subjects bow
> To a new-crowned monarch; such it is
> As are those dulcet sounds in break of day
> That creep into the dreaming bridegroom's ear,
> And summon him to marriage. Now he goes,
> With no less presence, but with much more love,
> Than young Alcides, when he did redeem
> The virgin tribute paid by howling Troy
> To the sea-monster. I stand for sacrifice;
> The rest aloof are the Dardanian wives,
> With bleared visages come forth to view
> The issue of th' exploit. Go, Hercules,
> Live thou, I live; with much, much more dismay
> I view the fight than thou that mak'st the fray.
>   (3.2.47–62)

If we desire to unlock the rich theological symbolism in these beautiful lines we need to remember the ecclesiological metaphor of the Bride and the Bridegroom that Shakespeare employs so often in his plays. Portia, as the desired bride, is a metaphor for the Church, the gate (*porta* in Latin) to heaven; Bassanio, as the bridegroom, is a metaphor for Christ and, by extension, a metaphor for Robert Southwell, who, as a priest, is *in persona Christi*, not merely during the Mass but in the very essence of his priesthood. Such symbolism is largely unknown to the modern reader or the postmodern critic, but it was most certainly not unknown to Shakespeare and his largely Catholic audience.

The metaphor is strengthened still further by its connection to the nature of the choice facing Bassanio. We know already, through the failure of the unworthy suitors to choose correctly, that he must spurn the follies of pride and the gaudiness of the world, and that he must embrace the death that awaits him in the lead-lined coffin in which is to be found his heart's desire and his true reward. He must choose death over life in order to attain the love of his life. This, of course, is the crux of the choice facing all Christians at all times, and the crux of the choice facing the persecuted Catholics of Elizabeth's England: "He who finds his life will lose it, and he who loses his life for my [Jesus'] sake will find it" (Mt 10:39).[18] The choice of death, or choosing to die to oneself, is the only way to obtain the fullness of life, the love of the Other beyond the self, the Beloved that every rational heart desires.

At this juncture it is important yet again to remind ourselves of the metadramatic role of Robert Southwell

---

[18] The whole of this chapter from Matthew's Gospel resonates powerfully with the moral drama of *The Merchant of Venice*.

throughout the drama. We have seen how the Jesuit's allusive presence is evident in many parts of the play, and most
particularly during the test of the caskets in which Bassanio's hazarding all he has is connected to Southwell's willingness to lay down his life for his love of Christ and his
Church. As we move to the courtroom scene Southwell's
ghostly presence passes from Bassanio to Antonio, as the
latter finds himself at the mercy of a merciless persecutor.
Several scholars have suggested a metadramatic connection
between Shylock, as a thinly veiled personification of a
Puritan, and Antonio, as an equally thinly veiled personification of a Jesuit.[19] Such a connection adds a crucial
allegorical dimension to the whole courtroom scene in
which Shakespeare effectively re-creates the trial of his friend,
Robert Southwell, so that it is presented from the true
vantage point of Belmont (Catholicism) and not from the
gutter perspective of Venice (Elizabethan state propa-
ganda). Once such a connection is made, the very "justice" demanded by Shylock becomes uncannily and
uncomfortably close to the "justice" meted out by Elizabeth's
court to Southwell. Shylock claims that he has a right to
cut a pound of flesh nearest to the heart of Antonio. It is
the law, written in the bond, and he demands that the law
be obeyed. In Robert Southwell's case, the law demanded
that Jesuit "traitors" should be hanged, drawn, and quartered. This involved the convicted "traitor" being hanged
by his neck but cut down before he lost consciousness. He
would then be cut open, while still alive, and his heart
and other internal organs removed. In Southwell's case, the

---

[19] See Pearce, *Through Shakespeare's Eyes*, for a fuller discussion of this
metadramatic connection and the scholarly work that underpins the discussion, particularly in chapters 1, 5, 9, and 10.

prosecutors did not only demand a pound of their victim's flesh, nearest his heart; they actually obtained it, physically removing the heart and casting it into the fire.

Considering the ghostly omnipresence of Robert Southwell throughout *The Merchant of Venice*, it is hard to see Portia's beautiful "quality of mercy" speech as anything but a plea to Queen Elizabeth that she should show mercy to the Jesuits whom her courts were regularly putting to bloody death (4.1.184–204). Perhaps these lines indicate that the play was written prior to Southwell's execution, though they could serve equally as a plaintive criticism, after the execution, of the absence of mercy that had been shown to the martyred priest.

The sheer depth and breadth of Southwell's allusive presence in *The Merchant of Venice* would lead any honest observer to look for such a presence in Shakespeare's other plays, particularly those written at around the same time. Since most scholars agree that *Romeo and Juliet* and *The Merchant of Venice* were both written in or around 1595 we might reasonably expect to see references to the Jesuit martyr or to his work in *Romeo and Juliet*.

In the first instance, it is apparent that the very theme of *Romeo and Juliet* dovetails with a recurring theme in Southwell's work that "lewd love is loss" and that true freedom is to be found in the purification of love through sanctity. We have already discussed how Southwell might have had Shakespeare's *Venus and Adonis* in mind when he complained that the "finest wits" write of Venus and her erotic wiles, thereby allowing their true Christian orientation to be clouded by the "misty loves" of Eros. We have also seen how Shakespeare's writing of *The Rape of Lucrece* might have been inspired by the desire to respond positively to Southwell's complaint, and how

certain critics have seen clear parallels between Shakespeare's *Lucrece* and Southwell's *St. Peter's Complaint*. Yet
surely *Romeo and Juliet*, of all Shakespeare's plays, is the
one that condemns most forthrightly the lewd love of eros
and its destructive consequences. Compare, for instance,
the way in which Shakespeare employs the imagery that
Southwell uses in praise of the Blessed Virgin as a means
of exposing the idolatrous nature of Romeo's love for Juliet.
Here is Southwell's praise of the Virgin:

> Her face a heaven, two planets were her eyes
> Whose gracious light did make our clearest day,
> But one such heaven there was, and lo it dies,
> Death's dark eclipse hath dimmed every ray.
> Sun hide thy light, thy beam's untimely shine,
> True light sith we have lost we crave not thine.[20]

And here is Romeo's praise of Juliet at the beginning of
the famous balcony scene:

> But, soft! What light through yonder window breaks?
> It is the east, and Juliet is the sun.
> Arise, fair sun, and kill the envious moon,
> Who is already sick and pale with grief
> That thou her maid art far more fair than she.
> Be not her maid, since she is envious;
> Her vestal livery is but sick and green,
> And none but fools do wear it; cast it off . . .
> Two of the fairest stars in all the heaven,
> Having some business, do entreat her eyes
> To twinkle in their spheres till they return.

[20] Southwell, "The Death of Our Lady", *Poems of Robert Southwell*, p. 12.
The spelling has been modernized in this and all the following citations of
Southwell's poetry.

What if her eyes were there, they in her head?
The brightness of her cheek would shame those stars,
As daylight doth a lamp; her eyes in heaven
Would through the airy region stream so bright
That birds would sing, and think it were not night.

(2.2.2–23)

In the midst of these idolatrous lines, which constitute an
infernal and inverted parody of Southwell's earlier poem
in praise of the Virgin, Romeo explicitly spurns virginity
as the "vestal livery" that "none but fools do wear". Romeo
desires that Juliet should cease to be a maid who wears
the virginal livery of Diana, the goddess of chastity, and
should instead sacrifice her virginity on the altar of the
voluptuous Venus, his own weapon being the sacrificial
knife.

In similar vein, the conflict between passion and reason
that forms the overarching dramatic tension of *Romeo and
Juliet* was the subject of Southwell's poem "Man's Civil War",
in which a slavish subservience to passion is shown to constitute an abandonment of reason and wisdom, and that such
abandonment brings destructive consequences:

> Where reason loathes, there fancy loves,
> And overrules the captive will,
> Foes senses are to virtue's lore,
> They draw the wit their wish to fill ...
>
> O cruel fight where fighting friend
> With love doth kill a favoring foe,
> Where peace with sense is war with God,
> And self delight the seed of woe,
>
> Dame pleasure's drugs are steeped in sin,
> Their sugared taste doth breed annoy,

> O fickle sense beware her gin,
> Sell not thy soul for brittle joy.[21]

Such is the harmony that exists between Southwell's cautionary verse and Shakespeare's cautionary play that the one could easily serve as an epigraph to the other. The same is true of another of Southwell's verse in which beauty is described as "a bait that swallowed choaks" and as a "treasure sought still to the owners' harms", whose "mortal charms" offer a "baleful bliss that damns where it delights":

> Where will doth wish, that wisdom doth reprove:
> Where nature craves, that grace must needs deny,
> Where sense doth like, that reason cannot love,
> Where best in show, in final proof is worst,
> Where pleasures upshot is to die accurst.[22]

Such is Southwell's preoccupation with the deadly lure of Venus, or venery, that it serves as the recurring motif of much of his verse, in much the way that it serves as the dominant motif in the love affair between Shakespeare's lovers. In his poem "At Home in Heaven", Southwell contrasts the spiritual beauty of the soul with the purely physical beauty of the body, entreating his readers to value the former over the fickleness of the latter:

> Give not assent to muddy minded skill,
> That deems the feature of a pleasing face
> To be the sweetest bait to lure the will:
> Not valuing right the worth of ghostly grace:
> Let God's and angels' censure win belief,
> That of all beauties judge our souls the chief.

---

[21] Southwell, "Man's Civil War", in *Poems of Robert Southwell*, p. 50.
[22] Southwell, "What Joy to Live", in *Poems of Robert Southwell*, p. 54.

Queen Hester was of rare and peerless hew,
And Judith once for beauty bare the vaunt,
But he that could our souls' endowments view,
Would soon to souls the crown of beauty grant.[23]

Southwell's poem "Love's Servile Lot" is so palpably pertinent to the moral thread with which Shakespeare weaves his tragedy that it almost serves as a commentary on the moral fabric of the play itself. Servile love separates will from wit, and the senses from reason; she is delightful on the surface but corrupt in the core:

> She shroudeth vice in virtue's veil,
> Pretending good in ill:
> She offreth joy, affordeth grief,
> A kiss where she doth kill.[24]

She binds the lovers "in tender twist", like fleas in a spider's web, and inflicts wounds like a tyrant, while offering, like a surgeon, to heal the pain she causes. Yet the pain and the comfort "have equal force, / For death is both their ends". She induces those in her thrall to throw themselves into the tempest of passion in defiance of reason:

> Moods, passions, fancy's jealous fits,
> Attend upon her train;
> She yieldeth rest without repose,
> A heav'n in hellish pain.

As we read these lines we see visions of Shakespeare's lovers throwing themselves to the ground in inconsolable grief-stricken tantrums, threatening suicide. And when we read

---

[23] Southwell, "At Home in Heaven," in *Poems of Robert Southwell*, p. 56.
[24] Southwell, "Love's Servile Lot," in *Poems of Robert Southwell*, pp. 60–62. Subsequent quotes of this poem are from this source.

the following verse we are haunted by the lovers' desperate
and suicidal end:

> Her sleep in sin, doth end in wrath,
> Remorse rings her awake,
> Death calls her up, shame drives her out,
> Despairs her upshot make.

The same theme is taken up by Southwell in "Lewd Love
Is Losse",[25] the poem to which Shakespeare seems to allude
in *The Merchant of Venice*. In this verse, as in so many others, the Jesuit poet cautions his readers not to fall into "fancy's
trap" or allow themselves to be lured by "gracious features" which "Lull reason's force asleep in error's lap, / Or
draw thy wit to bent of wanton's will". The latter part of
this poem is worth quoting in full, not only because it seems
to have influenced Shakespeare directly in his depiction of
the "lewd love" of those who failed Portia's casket test in
The Merchant of Venice but because it serves as a commentary on Shakespeare's theme in *Romeo and Juliet*:

> The fairest flowers have not the sweetest smell,
> A seeming heaven proves oft a damning hell.
>
> Self pleasing souls that play with beauty's bait,
> In shining shroud may swallow fatal hook.
> Where eager sight, or semblant fair doth wait,
> A lock it proves that first was but a look.
> The fish with ease into the net doth glide,
> But to get out, the way is not so wide.
>
> So long the fly doth dally with the flame,
> Until the singed wings do force his fall:

---

[25] See note 12 on p. 146 above. Subsequent quotes of this poem are from
this source.

So long the eye doth follow fancy's game,
Till love hath left the heart in heavy thrall.
Soon may the mind be cast in Cupid's jail,
But hard it is imprisoned thoughts to bail.

O loathe that love whose final aim is lust,
Moth of the mind, eclipse of reason's light:
The grave of grace, the mole of nature's rust,
The wracke of wit, the wrong of every right.
In sum and evil whose harms not tongue can tell,
In which to live is death, to die is hell.

There is perhaps further evidence of Southwell's influence on Shakespeare in general, and *Romeo and Juliet* in particular, in the punning connection between Romeo's exclamation after his fateful slaying of Tybalt that he is "fortune's fool" and the title of Southwell's poem "Fortune's Falsehood".[26] Yet again, Southwell's poem elucidates Shakespeare's theme. It commences with a description of the ways in which "sly fortune's subtleties" ensnare fortune's fools with "shrewd hooks" and "baits of happiness", wherein "misery" lurks amidst "worldly merriments". As the theme is developed, clear and applicable parallels with *Romeo and Juliet* become apparent. Fortune soothes appetites "with pleasing vanities", reminding us of the Petrarchan vanities and conceits with which Romeo initially wooed Juliet, but fortune uses such pleasing platitudes to conquer her victim "with cloaked tyranny". She opens "death's door" with "fawning flattery", alluring her fools "to bloody destiny", their subsequent ruin "registering her false felicity". Like the hapless

---

[26] Southwell, "Fortune's Falsehood", in *Poems of Robert Southwell*, p. 65. Subsequent quotes of this poem are from this source.

Romeo and Juliet, fortune's false "hopes are fastened in bliss that vanisheth".

A further and more direct connection between Shakespeare's play and Southwell's poem is to be found in the penultimate stanza of Southwell's verse in which the ways of fortune are described as "a labyrinth of wandering passages" in which fortune's "fools" take their "common pilgrimage to cursed deities". The link between fortune's falsehood in Southwell's poem and "fortune's fool" (Romeo) is evident in the way in which Romeo describes his lips as "two blushing pilgrims" in his very first words to Juliet. The profanity of the inappropriate religious imagery that he employs throughout the first exchange with Juliet testifies to the "cursed deities", which his words' "pleasing vanities" and "fawning flattery" serve. Through such flattery, "death's door" is opened, alluring Juliet "to bloody destiny".

Perhaps less obvious but nonetheless worthy of note is the possible connection between the "light love" to which Juliet yields and the love that "loveth light" to which Southwell refers in his poem "From Fortune's Reach".[27] Whereas "light love" is the unchaste or frivolous love of Venus, luring lovers to the "bloody destiny" of fortune's fools, the love that "loveth light" of which Southwell writes is the chaste love, the caritas, or agape, that enables one to love truly. The very theme of this particular poem is the stark contrast between "light love" and the love that "loveth light", illustrating how the former is the love into which fortune's fools "fall", whereas the latter, as the poem's title indicates, is the love that frees the lover "from fortune's reach". The scene is set in the opening verse:

[27] Southwell, "From Fortune's Reach", in *Poems of Robert Southwell*, pp. 66–67. Subsequent quotes of this poem are from this source.

Let fickle fortune run her blindest race:
I settled have an unremoved mind:
I scorn to be the game of fancy's chase,
Or vane to show the change of every wind.
Light giddy humors stinted to no rest,
Still change their choice, yet never choose the best.

Against this light giddy love that offers nothing but rest-
lessness, the poet chooses an altogether different love. He is
no slave to "beauty's fading bliss" but seeks and finds "a
light that ever shines" whose "glorious beams" will yield
his soul "the sum of all delights":

My light to love, my love to life doth guide
To life that lives by love, and loveth light.

Shakespeare may have had this poem in mind, with its
dizzying and dazzling play of words on "light", "love", and
"life", when he himself plays on the words of "light" and
"love" during the balcony scene. Romeo tells Juliet that he
had flown over the orchard walls "with love's light wings",
whereas Juliet, worrying that Romeo might find her behavior "light", i.e., immodest or unchaste, begs him to pardon
her "yielding to light love" (2.2.105). A few lines later, she
worries that their brazen forwardness is "too rash, too
unadvis'd, too sudden"; it is "too like the lightning, which
doth cease to be / Ere one can say 'It lightens'" (2.2.118–
20). Their love is so light that she fears that it will be as
blinding and as instantaneously spent as lightning itself. Her
words are indeed prophetic of the moral blindness that their
"light love" causes and the dazzling suddenness with which
it is spent. Their being struck with "light love" would prove
as sudden and as deadly as lightning itself. Compare this with
the "light that ever shines", which is the reward for the "life

that lives by love, and loveth light", far "from fortune's reach", to which the Jesuit refers. Such a comparison becomes even more apparent when we note the ubiquitous imagery of darkness throughout Shakespeare's play.

As we have seen and as we might have expected, Southwell's influence on Shakespeare is most evident in *The Merchant of Venice* and *Romeo and Juliet*, the plays that were written around the time of Southwell's martyrdom. There is, however, ample evidence of the Jesuit's ghostly presence in several of Shakespeare's other plays and poems.

We have already examined the evidence of Southwell's influence upon Shakespeare's early poetry, *Venus and Adonis* and *The Rape of Lucrece*, and several scholars have also illustrated the connection between Shakespeare's enigmatic and cryptic poem, "The Phoenix and the Turtle", and the plight of the English recusants and martyrs. Yet few critics seem to have connected Shakespeare's sonnet 73 with Southwell's "A Vale of Tears".[28] The line in the sonnet evoking the "bare ruin'd choirs, where late the sweet birds sang" is accepted by most critics as a melancholy allusion to the dissolution of England's monasteries in the wake of Henry VIII's destructive and self-serving "reformation", but few have seen the line's similarities to those of Southwell's evocation of "dales with stoney ruins strow'd":

> And in the horror of this fearful choir,
> Consists the music of this doleful place:
> All pleasant birds their tunes from thence retire,
> Where none but heavy notes have any grace.

---

[28] Southwell, "A Vale of Tears", in *Poems of Robert Southwell*, pp. 41–43. Subsequent quotes of this poem are from this source.

In both the sonnet and the poem, the "birds", sweet and pleasant, evoke the monks whose plainchant can no longer be heard in the midst of the choir's ruins. Whether Shakespeare's sonnet was inspired by Southwell's dirgeful lament or whether the similarities are merely coincidental, the poets' shared nostalgia for the passing of Catholic England is clear for all to see.

Another clear allusion to Southwell is offered by Shakespeare in the graveyard scene in *Hamlet*. In the short exchange with Horatio that follows the famous scene with the skull of Yorick we see a memento mori that offers further clear and present evidence of Shakespeare's friendship with the Jesuit. Holding the skull and asking Horatio whether the skull of Alexander the Great might have looked much the same when buried in the earth, Hamlet muses wistful on the fact that even the greatest men in history must return to dust:

> Alexander died, Alexander was buried, Alexander
> returneth to dust; the dust is earth; of earth we make
> loam; and why of that loam whereto he was converted
> might they not stop a beer-barrel?
> Imperious Caesar, dead and turn'd to clay,
> Might stop a hole to keep the wind away.
>
> (*Hamlet*, 5.1.203–8)

Many of Shakespeare's contemporaries must have seen the obvious allusion in Hamlet's discussion of Alexander and Caesar, within the context of a memento mori, with a verse from Robert Southwell's own famous poetic memento mori, "Upon the Image of Death":

> Though all the East did quake to hear
> Of Alexander's dreadful name,

> And all the West did likewise fear,
>   To hear of Julius Caesar's fame,
> Yet both by death in dust now lie,
>   Who then can scape but he must die?[29]

The Clown's claim earlier in the graveyard scene that "thou dost ill to say the gallows is built stronger than the church" (5.1.48–49) would appear to point to the plight of the English martyrs, such as Southwell, who were hanged, drawn, and quartered for the "crime" of being Catholic priests in Elizabeth's England. Which would prove stronger: The gallows or the Church? The hangman or the martyr? Machiavellian realpolitik or Christian principle? The "own self above all" secular politics of King Claudius, Polonius, Elizabeth, and William Cecil or the Christian convictions of Hamlet, Shakespeare, and Southwell?

In similar vein, Lear's deliriously happy words to Cordelia, the daughter to whom he has been reconciled, resonate with allusions to Southwell and the Jesuit martyrs:

> Come, let's away to prison:
> We two alone will sing like birds i' th' cage:
> When thou dost ask me blessing, I'll kneel down
> And ask of thee forgiveness: so we'll live,
> And pray, and sing, and tell old tales, and laugh
> At gilded butterflies, and hear poor rogues
> Talk of court news; and we'll talk with them too,
> Who loses and who wins, who's in, who's out;
> And take upon's the mystery of things,
> As if we were God's spies: and we'll wear out,

---

[29] Southwell, "Upon the Image of Death", in *Poems of Robert Southwell*, pp. 73–74.

> In a walled prison, packs and sects of great ones
> That ebb and flow by th' moon.
>
> (*King Lear*, 5.3.8–19)[30]

Lear gets his desire instantly, as Edmund orders them to be taken to prison. His response is one of joy: "Upon such sacrifices, my Cordelia, / The gods themselves throw incense" (5.3.20–21). It is indeed difficult to read these lines without the ghostly presence of martyred Catholics coming to mind. The Jesuits were "traitors" in the eyes of Elizabethan and Jacobean law but were "God's spies" in the eyes of England's Catholics. If caught they were imprisoned and tortured before being publicly executed. Since it seems likely that Shakespeare had known Southwell, and since it is even possible that he might have been amongst the large crowd who witnessed Southwell being executed, the words of Lear resonate with potent poignancy: "Upon such sacrifices . . . [t]he gods themselves throw incense." Within this context the repetition of the word "traitor" four times in only eighteen lines by Regan and Cornwall during their interrogation of Gloucester earlier in the play has added significance. It is also significant perhaps that Edmund declares himself a disciple of the new secular creed of Machiavelli almost immediately after these words of Lear are spoken. "[K]now thou this, that men / Are as the time is" (5.3.31–32), he declares, implicitly deriding the "madness" of Lear's faith-driven words in favor of relativism and self-serving realpolitik. Lear had himself criticized the Machiavellian worldliness of Edmund and his ilk in his stated desire that he and Cordelia, from the sanity and sanctity of their prison cell, should "laugh at

---

[30] All quotes from *King Lear* are taken from William Shakespeare, *King Lear*, ed. Joseph Pearce, Ignatius Critical Editions (San Francisco: Ignatius Press, 2008).

gilded butterflies", those elaborately attired courtiers flut-
tering over nothing but fads and fashions, "and hear poor
rogues talk of court news", in the knowledge that they as
"God's spies" will outlast, even in "a walled prison", the
"packs and sects of great ones" which "ebb and flow by th'
moon". Fashions come and go, Lear seems to be saying,
but the Truth remains. He also seems to be implying, through
his reference to the moon, that it is Edmund and the play's
other "gilded butterflies" and "poor rogues" who are the
real lunatics, trading the promise of virtue's eternal reward
for life's transient pleasures, trading sanity for the madness
of Machiavelli.

All of this would have been deducible enough without
the deliberate connection to Southwell's poetry that Shakespeare embeds cryptically in the midst of Lear's politically
charged words. We have seen how the phrase "God's spies"
would have been seen as a reference to the Jesuits, at least
in the eyes of the Catholics in Shakespeare's audience, but
the connection becomes unmistakable when connected with
Southwell's poem "Decease Release".[31] This poem, written in the first person with Mary Stuart, Queen of Scots,
as the narrator, refers to the executed queen as "pounded
spice":

> The pounded spice both taste and scent doth please,
> In fading smoke the force doth incense show,
> The perished kernel springeth with increase,
> The lopped tree doth best and soonest grow.
>
> God's spice I was and pounding was my due,
> In fading breath my incense savored best,

---

[31] Southwell, "Decease Release", *Poems of Robert Southwell*, pp. 47–48. Subsequent quotes of this poem are from this source.

Death was the mean my kernel to renew,
By lopping shot I up to heavenly rest.

Although the poem is clearly Southwell's tribute to the
executed Queen of Scots, its being written in the first person gave it added potency following Southwell's own execution. Like the martyred queen of whom he wrote, Southwell
was also "pounded spice" whose essence is more pleasing
and valued for being crushed: "God's spice I was and pound-
ing was my due". As a Jesuit in Elizabethan England, Southwell had been one of "God's spies" who, being caught,
became "God's spice", ground to death that he might receive
his martyr's reward in heaven. "Upon such sacrifices," Shakespeare exclaims through the lips of Lear, "the gods themselves throw incense" (5.3.20–21).

INDEX